dreamality

BOB COY

At the age of twenty-four, Bob Coy left an executive position in the music industry to serve as an associate pastor with Calvary Chapel of Las Vegas. In 1985 Bob and his wife, Diane, moved to South Florida and began Calvary Chapel of Fort Lauderdale. As senior pastor he has become well known for his unique style in expounding the Scriptures, making them come alive, and relating them to those of us living in the twenty-first century. His teaching style emphasizes life application of the highest standards of God's truth, while his delivery captures the loving heart of God's Spirit. Pastor Bob has had the rare privilege of watching God's miraculous hand in the individual lives of those in the fellowship and in the corporate body as a whole. From the first meeting in a living room with four in attendance, Calvary Chapel Fort Lauderdale has become home to over seventeen thousand men and women from the tri-county area and ranks eighth on the list of fastest growing churches in the country. Though many have tried to attribute the rapid growth to numerous reasons, no one is more surprised by the phenomenon than Pastor Bob Coy, who gives the total credit and glory to God alone.

dream*ality*

heaven's dream – your reality

BOB COY

OUR PURPOSE AT HOWARD PUBLISHING IS TO:
- Increase faith in the hearts of growing Christians
- Inspire holiness in the lives of believers
- Instill hope in the hearts of struggling people everywhere
BECAUSE HE'S COMING AGAIN!

Dreamality © 2005 by Bob Coy
All rights reserved. Printed in the United States of America
Published by Howard Publishing Co., Inc.
3117 North Seventh Street, West Monroe, LA 71291-2227
www.howardpublishing.com

05 06 07 08 09 10 11 12 13 14   10 9 8 7 6 5 4 3 2 1

Edited by Between the Lines
Interior design by John Mark Luke Designs
Cover design by David Carlson
Photography by Getty Images

Library of Congress Cataloging-in-Publication Data
Coy, Bob, 1955–
    Dreamality : heaven's dream-your reality / Bob Coy.
        p. cm.
    Includes bibliographical references.
    ISBN 1-58229-447-X
    1. Dreams—Religious aspects—Christianity. 2. Joseph (Son of Jacob) 3. Christian life.
I. Title.

BR115.D74C96 2005
234'.25—dc22

                                                            2005046303

Scripture quotations not otherwise marked are taken from the *New King James Version*®. Copyright © 1982 by Thomas Nelson, Inc. Used by permission. All rights reserved. Scripture quotations marked ICB are taken from the *International Children's Bible, New Century Version* © 1986, 1988 by Word Publishing, Nashville, TN 37214. Used by permission. Scripture quotations marked KJV are taken from *The Holy Bible, Authorized King James Version*. Scripture quotations marked "The Message" are taken from *The Message*. Copyright © 1993, 1994, 1995, 1996, 2000, 2001, 2002. Used by permission of NavPress Publishing Group. All rights reserved. Scripture quotations marked NIV are taken from the *Holy Bible, New International Version*®. Copyright © 1973, 1978, 1984 by International Bible Society. Used by permission of Zondervan. All rights reserved. Scripture quotations marked NLT are taken from the *Holy Bible, New Living Translation*, copyright © 1996. Used by permission of Tyndale House Publishers, Inc., Wheaton, Illinois 60189. All rights reserved.

It is God who gives dreams, and this book is no exception. From the first glimmer of possibility to the last letter on the page, this book has been an illustration of how an almighty God can work in and through mere men and women to accomplish a dream beyond the imagination of any of the team. So, from all of us who co-labored on this project, we want to extend a heartfelt thanks to our Lord Jesus Christ for saving us from even the best self-driven dreams for the more excellent God-given one that He is still orchestrating in our lives at this very moment.

And I am sure that God, who began the good work within you, will continue his work until it is finally finished on that day when Christ Jesus comes back again. (Philippians 1:6 NLT)

contents

prologue: i want my dreams *back* 1

introduction: everybody *dreams* 5

Part One: Heaven's *Dream*

1: the heart behind the *dream* 13

2: provision to *share* 33

3: power to *save* 49

4: position to *shine* 73

Part Two: Hell's *Nightmare*

5: the hate behind the *nightmare* 93

6: the *pit* 113

7: the *marketplace* 129

8: the *prison* 151

Part Three: Our *Reality*

9: dreams *redeemed* 173

10: an abundant *dream* 191

11: a supernatural *dream* 207

12: an excellent *dream* 225

epilogue 239

notes 241

i want my dreams *back*

"Oh, Daddy," sobbed my normally cheerful four-year-old daughter. Then with a frustration bordering on anger, she blurted out, "You took my dream away!"

"Caitlyn, what do you mean?"

"Daddy," she explained in exasperation, "I was having the greatest dream. It was beautiful, and then you came in and woke me up."

And with an intensity that left me pondering the deeper, more universal aspect of her cry, she exclaimed, "Daddy, I want my dreams back!"

I understood all too well my daughter's feeling. We've all had times in our lives when our dreams are better than our reality. Then the alarm clock sounds, bringing us back to another day—a routine commute, a boring job, a mundane schedule, a mediocre life, and the haunting fear that none of it is really worthwhile. That's when we, too, want to lament, "I want my dreams back!"

Caitlyn's tiny face, all scrunched up in despair, and her childlike request melted my heart and resonated in a deep part of my spirit. She herself was the fulfillment of a dream God had given back to my wife

1

and me. When Diane and I married, we hadn't really talked about when we would have kids. Like many couples, we took it for granted that at some point we would begin a family. That assumption would prove to be one we had mistakenly made.

We moved to Fort Lauderdale in 1985 to start a Calvary Chapel church, and for the first few years our focus and our dreams were centered on this endeavor. But as time passed, we began to think we were ready to take on the challenge of raising kids. After trying for six or seven years with no success, we were forced to admit there might be a problem, and we went to a fertility specialist. We did not yet know that we were in the middle of what would be an eleven-year journey from the time we first tried to get pregnant until the birth of our first child. This venture of faith was comprised of prayer; testing (diagnostic and spiritual); emotional roller-coaster rides of yes we are, no we are not pregnant, should we adopt or shouldn't we; and a draining of financial resources—all of which ultimately forced us to trust God beyond the limits of our own understanding.

Psalm 30:5 says, "Weeping may endure for a night, but joy comes in the morning." After a long night of weeping, our first child, a son, was born one joyful morning in October 1995.

We had been proud parents less than a year when we discovered that Diane was pregnant again. We were elated until, three months into the pregnancy, we lost the baby. Horrible as that loss was, we then had to face the fact that we might never be able to have another child. That possibility was devastating.

The next two years seemed like an eternity of endless prayers, asking God to restore our hope of a second child. Then our daughter, Caitlyn, was born. Perhaps that's why the sight of my daughter's precious face asking for her dreams back made me realize that her request must echo again and again in the halls of heaven. As an earthly dad, I didn't have the resources or power to accomplish such a supernatural thing as giving Caitlyn back her dream. But our heavenly Father is all powerful, all knowing, and present in any and every situation in which someone, in frustration or even anger, cries out, "I want my dreams back!" And God is a good, kind, benevolent Father who wants to restore our dreams.

Somewhere between childhood and adulthood, we let go of our dreams. What we dared to imagine and ask for as kids seems silly and unrealistic as grownups. We stop trusting that things can be different. We stop hoping that things will get better. We stop expecting life to be full of excitement, anticipation, joy, fun, and hope. When we do dare to dream of something more, we often experience instead the stagnation of the status quo.

So we let go of our dreams in exchange for the dream world of Hollywood and Madison Avenue. Instead of holding out for real friends, we settle for the sitcom *Friends*. And the result is that we are becoming increasingly angry and frustrated by the realization that life doesn't seem to work.

That's why I wrote this book. I hope to rekindle in your heart the expectation of something more. That's what we were created for— something more, something supernatural that is bigger than this world. It may seem like a dream long forgotten, but I pray that through the pages of this book, you'll regain the hope and beauty of the grand dream for your life that began in God's heart. Our heavenly Daddy wants His dream back too, and you are that dream.

everybody *dreams*

Who hasn't had a dream? Whether it's a four-year-old's desire to be a cowboy or a fifty-year-old's hope to spend the golden years on a beach, we all dream.

The human heart beats to dream and to hope. Some of our dreams are still on the horizon. Maybe we'd love to share life with someone special—sunset walks, honest talks, holding hands, sharing secrets—but that someone is nowhere in sight. Or perhaps we've already found that person, and our dream is to have a happy marriage in which ideas are exchanged and purpose is discovered. Others might dream of having kids—or obedient children. We may dream of an important promotion, a great accomplishment, an upcoming vacation, being old enough to drive, or graduating from high school, college, or medical school. The variety of dreams is as countless as our thoughts.

Yet all these and more can be summed up in humanity's hope to lead meaningful lives filled with purpose that transcends our own finite existence. It is this common bond of aspiration that causes our eyes to tear, our hearts to melt, and our determination to rise when we see others' dreams fulfilled.

Our Quest for Greatness

Part of us knows instinctively that God's plans for us are bigger, grander, and more meaningful than any plans we could make, and the cry of our hearts for greatness makes us identify with people like Eric Liddell in *Chariots of Fire*. Eric was a famous runner from Scotland who refused to run in his best event, the one-hundred-meter race, at the Paris Olympics in the summer of 1924 because the heats were held on Sunday. He chose to run in the four-hundred-meter competition instead, a race he was not expected to win. The Flying Scotsman, as he was affectionately called, won a gold medal in that race and set a new world record.[1] As depicted in the movie *Chariots of Fire*, Liddell made this profound statement: "I believe God made me for a purpose, but he also made me fast, and when I run I feel God's pleasure."[2] He was living in the reality of heaven's dream and sensed that God was pleased with him. He was doing the thing he was created to do, loved best, and excelled at most. And we experience the thrill of victory through his story.

We're driven to our feet, cheering, when the long shot wins the race or when Rocky comes back from a beating that would kill the average man to take the world championship in boxing. We're wired for victory.

How did we get that way? The Bible tells us that God made us in His own image. That's one reason we dream. God is into dreams. He's the dream distributor and the dream deliverer: God is in the business of giving us dreams and then fulfilling those dreams in our lives.

Before I go much further, I feel compelled to clarify this point. I don't want my voice to be thrown in with the voices that would make God a cosmic genie. I'm not focusing on health, wealth, and prosperity. I'm not talking about self-centered hype but about holy, godly hope. The kind of dream I'm referring to is not a myopic, selfish abstraction from God born out of flesh; it's a spiritual aspiration toward God born out of faith. I'm talking about why God created each of us as we are and about the realization of His purpose in our lives.

For instance, why did God make Thomas Edison the way He did? Have you ever wondered why this man had such insatiable curiosity about electricity? Who gave him the perseverance to harness the power of nature and light the way of mankind? Or who gave Henry Ford the idea for an assembly line? What about the Wright brothers and their airplane? Or Bill Gates and his computer-programming ideas? As we look back through history and at modern-day marvels and then delve into our own dusty daydreams, it becomes apparent that in the heart of every human lies a dream.

Chosen Children

The Bible is rich with accounts of God-given dreams. Whether through Abraham and his family, Esther and her destiny, David and the temple, or Joshua and the Promised Land, we see God giving and fulfilling dreams.

This book will take a closer look at biblical dreams through the life of a young dreamer named Joseph. We'll see why some dreams go nowhere while others blossom. Once we've completed this journey with Joseph, I'm sure we'll believe not only in God-given dreams but also in the God who loves us deeply. Only He can say to us, with the ability to deliver, "You can have your dreams back, because they were made with you in mind!"

Let's pick up Joseph's story in Genesis 37: "Israel loved Joseph more than all his children, because he was the son of his old age. Also he made him a tunic of many colors. But when his brothers saw that their father loved him more than all his brothers, they hated him and could not speak peaceably to him."

If we're going to grasp the importance of Joseph's life in relation to ours, we'll need to look at some of the stark parallels between Joseph and us and what they reveal about our position as Christians. Each of us is, as Joseph was, a favorite child. Jesus said, "You did not choose Me, but I chose you and appointed you that you should go and bear fruit, and that your fruit should remain, that whatever you ask the Father in My name He may give you" (John 15:16).

Christians are a selected seed—a chosen people. I realize that some will read this statement and think I'm being presumptuous. Perhaps, but it happens to be the truth. I don't want to have an attitude of arrogance or pride, but I do want to sincerely say that as Christians we can look at our lives with a sense of promise. Based on Scripture, we know we have a destiny to fulfill, and we understand that our heavenly Father favors us.

Just as Jacob loved Joseph in a special way, God loves each Christian in a special way. Each of us is unique in God's sight. For this reason, if we've had a dream and it has been dashed, God wants to resurrect that dream and breathe new life into it—just like, as we'll see, He did for Joseph.

The Battleground

Joseph set out in life with a dream, but along the way he encountered opposition:

Now Joseph had a dream, and he told it to his brothers; and they hated him even more. So he said to them, "Please hear this dream which I have dreamed: There we were, binding sheaves in the field. Then behold, my sheaf arose and also stood upright; and indeed your sheaves stood all around and bowed down to my sheaf." And his brothers said to him, "Shall you indeed reign over us? Or shall you indeed have dominion over us?" So they hated him even more for his dreams and for his words. (Genesis 37:5–8)

We all have dreams similar to Joseph's—dreams that say we're important, we belong to something bigger than our own lives, and we were meant for greatness. But what happens to those dreams along the road of life? How do we change from hopeful dreamers into disappointed or dutiful doers stuck in the rut of routine? The answer is, we have an adversary—a dream destroyer. And when he attacks, the life we thought would be a dream becomes a nightmare.

Sometimes we even lose the dream. And after a while, it becomes so long since we dared to believe in our dream that even talking about it makes us uneasy. We give in to the give-up spirit. We believe that dreams aren't real, that reality is this dreamless world in which the good guys finish last and the bad guys always win.

That's what the adversary wants us to believe. But it's a lie.

If we're going to fight for our dreams, we need to know who our real enemy is and what his strategies are. Ephesians 6:12 tells us, "Our fight is not against people on earth. We are fighting against the rulers and authorities and the powers of this world's darkness. We are fighting against the spiritual powers of evil in the heavenly world" (ICB).

Our battleground is in the arena of the unseen. Our foe is a master of dissuasion, and he often accomplishes this by offering earthly wisdom in place of divine oracle.

Many of us have had an experience like Joseph's. We had a dream and shared it with someone else only to have that person attack it: "Oh, you and your big dreams! Get a life, why don't you." But Joseph's dream wasn't just his—it was God's. God had given it to him based on who he had created Joseph to be. And so it is with us.

How many times have we said, "I wonder if I could . . ." Did we follow that dream or let ourselves be talked out of it?

Think about the first guy to dream about bottled water. He's with his buddy watching a babbling brook of clear water, and he says, "What if you actually bottled this water and sold it?" His buddy responds with what seems like sound human wisdom: "You've got to be kidding me— it's free! No one would pay a nickel for a bottle of water."

Oh really? At the ballpark just a few weeks ago, I paid $3.50 for a bottle of water—and the vendor kept selling out and having to run back for more. But what if the guy with the dream had listened to his friend who told him it was a stupid idea? Maybe today he'd be watching his dream being accomplished by someone else, and thinking, *That was my dream!*

That's exactly what happens when we don't understand that God is the dream deliverer and that He delights in fulfilling His dreams in and through us because we are His children.

If we don't know God's heart toward us, and if we don't grasp the concept of a bigger picture, we can easily be deceived, become disappointed, and let go of our dreams when we encounter obstacles. But God has given each of us a dream. And it's time, with His help, to live it. When we do, we will be living a "dreamality"—a life that manifests God's purpose and design. Heaven's dream will have become our reality.

Part One

Heaven's *Dream*

the heart behind the *dream*

Before we can fully appreciate and capture heaven's dream, we'll need to get a clearer view of the Dreamer Himself. We have dreams because we are created in the image of God, who dreamed up the whole human race in the first place. And God wants to see our dreams fulfilled. But because we're created in God's image, we can dream all on our own. So how are we to know if our dreams are God-given or self-driven?

The story of Joseph sheds much light on this subject of dreams. Early in life Joseph had a God-given dream that he would be a significant player in the game of life. Yet as time unfolded, his dream met with the same kinds of obstacles and challenges that ours often do. Joseph was forced to evaluate and determine whether his dream truly was from God or whether it was something he'd thought up on his own. He also was faced with the same question we are when our dreams hit those inevitable bumps in the road: is the dream worth the fight to keep it alive?

Although Joseph's was a literal, while-he-was-sleeping dream, it bears some profound similarities to the life dreams we'll discuss in this book. In the same way that Joseph's dream was from the Lord and contained three specific components, so our life dreams are from the Lord and will display those same ingredients that are part of all God-given dreams: the provision to share, the power to save, and the position to shine. We'll explore these three areas in greater detail, but first we need to do a little soul searching and ask ourselves, do we really want God's dreams for our lives? Our answer to this question will determine our success or failure in the quest for our dreamality.

A Biblical View of God

Wanting God's dreams for our lives necessitates trusting God with our lives. So before we answer the above question, it behooves us to look more closely at just whom we would be trusting. Allow me to offer a brief introduction of God. For some readers who have grown up with an understanding of God, this may seem insulting. I don't want to offend anyone, but neither do I want to miss the opportunity to address the primary reason so many of us settle for self-driven dreams when we could enjoy the pursuit of God-given dreams.

One of the most heartbreaking discoveries I've made in my years as a pastor is that most people do not know God. They know of Him, but they don't know Him. He has been painted in endless erroneous caricatures, ranging from an indulgent grandpa in the sky to a meanspirited taskmaster who waits for us to make a mistake so He can punish us. Yet our concept of God has a direct bearing on our ability to trust Him in this critical area of dreams.

Whoever and wherever we are in life, we will benefit from the view of God presented in the Bible. In His Word, God chose to call Himself our Father. To begin to understand God as our Father, it helps to think of what it means to us, as humans, to be parents.

As a father I have a love for my children that is beyond measure. I have hopes, aspirations, and desires for their accomplishments, their well-being, and their future. As a father who is human, I also have faults and flaws; I am subject to a sinful nature that can hinder my ability to parent well. God, on the other hand, is the perfect Father who has complete knowledge of all His children. He has no error or evil in Him. To think that I could do a better job at parenting than God does is insane, but to think that God would be any less good to me than I would be to my kids seems blasphemous. In fact, Jesus addressed this very audacity: "If a son asks for bread from any father among you, will he give him a stone? Or if he asks for a fish, will he give him a serpent instead of a fish? Or if he asks for an egg, will he offer him a scorpion? If

> So many of us settle for self-driven dreams when we could enjoy the pursuit of God-given dreams.

you then, being evil, know how to give good gifts to your children, how much more will your heavenly Father give the Holy Spirit to those who ask Him!" (Luke 11:11–13).

What parent can imagine saying, when his or her child asks for something to eat, "Sure, here are some rocks, serpents, and scorpions for breakfast. Enjoy." How absurd! We would never do that to our kids. In this passage of Scripture, Jesus said that although compared with God we're relatively evil, not even we would do something this wicked to our children. The implied question is, How then can we think that God— who is good, gracious, kind, benevolent, merciful, and righteous— would do something cruel or harmful to us, His children?

Luke 11 tells us that God knows what we're like. He knows we're naturally inclined to do things that are wrong, fleshly, unwise, and selfish. Yet even with that propensity, even with our flawed nature, look at how we love our kids. Look at how we want the best for them and how we'll defend them and be by their sides no matter what they do. It is as if God wants to hold our faces in His hands and say, "Look at me! Look at who I am. Am I not good? Am I not great? Am I not gracious?"

God's Goodness

The Bible goes to great lengths to express God's goodness. Consider these verses as a starting point:

- *"Oh, give thanks to the LORD, for He is good! For His mercy endures forever." (1 Chronicles 16:34)*

- *"Why do you boast in evil, O mighty man? The goodness of God endures continually." (Psalm 52:1)*

- *"Do you despise the riches of His goodness, forbearance, and longsuffering, not knowing that the goodness of God leads you to repentance?" (Romans 2:4)*

- *"The LORD God, merciful and gracious, longsuffering, and abounding in goodness and truth, keeping mercy for thousands, forgiving iniquity and transgression and sin." (Exodus 34:6–7)*

These are just a few of the many references to God's goodness in Scripture. Volumes have been written on the goodness of God. Every breath we take, every heartbeat, every sunrise, every newborn baby, every star in the universe, and much, much more tell of God's goodness. From a heavenly perspective, God's goodness is without question. It is only in the fuzzy focus of human understanding that His goodness becomes questionable. Throughout this book we will start to see how this happens, but for the sake of our introduction of God, let the record reflect that, beyond all doubt, He is good.

God's Greatness

God's greatness is seen in each and every aspect of the physical world in which we live. From the majesty of the universe to the intricacy of each atom, we witness the magnitude of our Creator. Scientists have discovered soil on Mars that has properties unlike any other they've seen, which has defied our previous understanding that we have only a finite number of elements in the universe. Think about how big that makes God. An entire planet out there is uninhabited—it's just the red star in the sky—but it's completely unparalleled to anything we have on Earth.

As human beings we're limited in our ability to create by the finite number of media with which we have to work. We can only mix and use so many colors to create art. We can only combine so many angles and curves to form architectural wonders. God has no such limitations. The Bible tells us, "Abraham believed in the God who brings the dead back to life and who brings into existence what didn't exist before" (Romans 4:17 NLT). The fact that we find soil made of elements we never knew of before is just one astounding display of God's enormous and endless capacity to create. He could have made Mars from the same elements as those of Earth, but He didn't. God has no limits.

God's Graciousness

God's graciousness is demonstrated in His mercy. The Bible tells us in Romans 3:23 that we all fall short of God's original plan. We're all guilty, and our guilt requires punishment—damnation for all eternity (see Isaiah 53:6; Romans 6:23). But God's parent-heart breaks at the thought of meting out such punishment. Still, God's perfect justice requires the full measure of judgment. That's why He had to send Jesus to take the penalty for our sin: "Christ had no sin. But God made him become sin. God did this for us so that in Christ we could become right with God" (2 Corinthians 5:21 ICB). Because of the punishment Jesus took on our behalf, God can righteously stand in the court of the universe and dole out mercy. In spite of the foolish and criminal things we've done, God, the righteous judge, can adjudicate us innocent because the punishment for our crime has been borne by Christ.

Humanity stands amazed at God's grace, and well it should. Think about the incredible love it must have taken to conceive of grace. It's a concept that's uniquely God's. Only through grace can He love us in spite of our sinful state. Grace is God saying, "I knew you'd behave badly, so I came up with a remedy." The Bible puts it this way: "Where sin increased, grace increased all the more, so that, just as sin reigned in death, so also grace might reign through righteousness to bring eternal life through Jesus Christ our Lord" (Romans 5:20–21 NIV).

In God's foreknowledge He knew that with the free will He had given humanity, they would disobey Him. Through this disobedience, sin entered the world, and with it came death (see Romans 5:12). Grace is God's way for us to escape the effects of sin. That's why Scripture tells us that we are saved through grace: "It is by grace you have been saved, through faith—and this not from yourselves, it is the gift of God—not by works, so that no one can boast" (Ephesians 2:8–9 NIV).

An Eternal Course

Even with God's gracious Father-heart toward us, we still can be intent on doing our own thing. We become consumed in a self-driven dream instead of enjoying the pursuit of a God-given dream and the blessing of doing His will.

Jesus said, "I am the vine, you are the branches. He who abides in Me, and I in him, bears much fruit; for without Me you can do nothing" (John 15:5). Some people may not be sure they believe that. After all, many great things have been done by people who didn't know Jesus. Empires have been established, corporations have been built from the ground up, people have gone to the moon—from time immemorial human beings have accomplished amazing feats of talent, bravery, and intelligence.

True, we've succeeded at many things as a human race, but there's a great divide between success and significance. We may have created something for our own glory, but every effort apart from God is merely temporal.

We, on the other hand, are eternal. Our lives are eternal. The journeys we're taking here on Earth are simply series of races. Some of the races are sprints—we'll learn a lesson quickly and move on. Others are marathons—we'll rid ourselves of some fleshly desires only through perseverance and endurance. Whatever the training, teaching, molding, or shaping, our courses are for an everlasting purpose. They can take us in one of two directions, but the path is eternal: "These people will go off to be punished forever. But the good people will go to live forever" (Matthew 25:46 ICB). That's why it's critical that we align our courses with heaven's dream, which will lead us into eternal life rather than eternal death.

Along with incorrect perceptions of God, many people have incorrect perceptions of eternal life. Those of us who reach heaven won't just sit around playing harps. We'll be assigned cosmic responsibilities. That's the implication of Jesus's words in the parable of the talents: "His master replied, 'Well done, good and faithful servant! You have been faithful with a few things; I will put you in charge of many things. Come and share your master's happiness!'" (Matthew 25:21 NIV).

Our lives as human beings span so much more than our brief existence on earth. The Bible tells us that the lives we live here are like vanishing vapor: "You do not know what will happen tomorrow! Your life is like a mist. You can see it for a short time, but then it goes away" (James 4:14 ICB). It's foolish to put all our hopes, dreams, and aspirations into our time here on Earth when it's just a drop in the bucket compared with our eternal existence.

God dwells in eternity. He is the God of all ages and of every generation: "My righteousness will be forever, and My salvation from generation to generation" (Isaiah 51:8). "You, O LORD, remain forever; Your throne from generation to generation" (Lamentations 5:19).

Just as God is eternal, so God-given dreams are eternal. If we're going to pursue heaven's dreams for our lives, we have to abandon the mind-set that sees our existence as date of birth to date of death, the end. In God's eyes our lives go from date of birth through date of departure from this world, the beginning of forever. That makes everything we do in the here and now pertinent to everything we will do after our time on earth. What we do here determines whether we enjoy eternity with God or suffer it without Him.

This concept of eternity is important because the dreams God puts in our hearts, that our Father wants to accomplish in us, are not just for the here and now. They extend to His kingdom in eternity. The story of Moses is a perfect illustration.

Moses was adopted by the daughter of Pharaoh. The entire temporal world of his day was at his fingertips, yet he felt a burden to see the nation of Israel set free. In his frustration over the Hebrews' plight, he tried to deliver them. But his own fleshly effort led him to kill an Egyptian.

I can picture God looking on and saying, "This is not how you fulfill the dream, Moses. You need to humble yourself and be my spokesperson for deliverance." As we look at the conversation that took place between them at the burning bush in the third chapter of Exodus, we see Moses making every excuse under the sun why he couldn't do what God was asking him to do. He just kept repeating, "I can't, I can't, I can't." Then, the Bible says, "The anger of the LORD was kindled against Moses" (Exodus 4:14). Not a good place to be.

> By not stepping into the roles for which we were made, we blow our only chances at complete satisfaction.

Why was God angry? As we look at Moses's life, it's easy to see the cause of God's frustration with him. God had saved Moses when all other Hebrew baby boys were being put to death. God not only spared

Moses's life, but He also arranged for him to be raised in Pharaoh's home, be nursed by his own mother, and receive an above-average education— all for the sake of this moment of commission at the burning bush. For Moses to say no at this point was just not acceptable. His existence was part of a master plan—a plan that would deliver an entire nation and bring personal blessing and purpose to Moses's life beyond any temporal accolades or riches. His life was a vital link in the plan that would ultimately bring salvation for all of mankind by preserving the lineage through which Christ the Redeemer was to come.

Our Eternal Plan

It is the same for us: our existence is part of a master plan. But when we are confronted with our roles in the master plan and say we can't or won't participate, what we're really refusing is the authority and providence of God in our lives. And our rejection ruins everything God has planned for us. By not stepping into the roles for which we were made, we blow our only chances at complete satisfaction. We're like cars that have decided to become bicycles. It doesn't make any sense. The car was created for a specific purpose, and so are we:

- *"God has made us what we are. In Christ Jesus, God made us new people so that we would do good works. God had planned in advance those good works for us. He had planned for us to live our lives doing them." (Ephesians 2:10 ICB)*

- *"'I know what I have planned for you,' says the Lord. 'I have good plans for you. I don't plan to hurt you. I plan to give you hope and a good future.'" (Jeremiah 29:11 ICB)*

When we resist the Creator, we miss out on the plans He created for us before time began. We will never know the satisfaction of fulfilling our purposes, because we'll miss the very things for which we were designed. When we settle for self-driven dreams, we settle for dreams that are but vapors.

Where is Moses today? He has responsibilities in the kingdom of God that are commensurate with the purpose and plan God had for his life—not just for his days on earth but for eternity as well. Moses's responsibilities are also based on his obedience in sticking with God's plan. Imagine if Moses had said, "You know what, the whole idea of wandering in the wilderness for forty years isn't really cutting it with me. I mean, I still own a chariot. I have a great place to hang out in Egypt if I want to. I can still build empires for Pharaoh. Hey, maybe I could compromise and do a little bit of an Egyptian thing and a little bit of Hebrew thing." Think about the absurdity of Moses's trying to live in both worlds.

A friend of mine recently said, "I continue to hear references to a Christian attorney, a Christian musician, a Christian businessman, etc. Whatever happened to just a Christian—you know, a person who forsakes everything from the world to do the thing God has called him or her to do?" Someone who says, "I'm so disconnected from what I used to do and be, that I have become a tool in God's hand to accomplish whatever He wants, because I've realized that this is the only way I will experience true and lasting fulfillment."

Why do we insist that we're "Christian musicians" or "musicians that are Christian"? Why can't we just be Christians—period? Why can't we let go of what our identities were before we knew Jesus? Perhaps we need to skip the music thing altogether. "No!" some might object. "That's my platform." Well, it may be your platform, but for how long? Was Moses an Egyptian deliverer? When do we say good-bye completely to Egypt for the sake of eternity?

A vocation can be a platform, but if the vocation becomes the identifier, it may be time to shift the identity. What is Moses known for? Was he Pharaoh's adopted grandson or God's deliverer? If we're really going to fulfill the dreams God has for our eternity, at some point we need to be willing to forsake our self-driven dreams and vocational identities for the sake of God's dreams and His image. I may not be acknowledged as a pastor in heaven. I hope to be known as a man who loved God as much as he could and was willing to do whatever God asked and go wherever He directed.

In 1985 I moved to Fort Lauderdale, Florida, to start a Calvary Chapel church. I had been an assistant pastor at Calvary Chapel Las Vegas and enjoyed the responsibility of teaching four hundred to five hundred people a week. After two years in Fort Lauderdale, still only thirty to fifty people a week attended the church. I was disheartened and began to long for the former days in Las Vegas. I decided to call Pastor Chuck Smith, founder of the Calvary Chapel movement. In a conversation with the man at Pastor Chuck's church who over saw the Calvary Chapel outreaches, I expressed my doubt and discouragement. I told him I was thinking about leaving Fort Lauderdale and going back to Las Vegas.

I was shocked at his response. He basically said, "That's fine, Bob. You can do that. I have about twenty Bible-college students who would love the opportunity to take over your small church." I hung up the phone knowing that God had handed me a choice: I could pursue my own self-driven dream of going back to the familiar life in Las Vegas where I pastored a congregation who knew and loved me, or I could accept heaven's dream, which had been birthed in prayer, to start a Calvary Chapel for a fellowship of believers in Fort Lauderdale.

A week or so later, as I drove down I-95 and was listening to Greg Laurie on the radio, God spoke to me through Greg's message. In my own kind of burning-bush-via-radio experience, I felt God saying, "Why don't you bloom where you're planted?"

It struck such a deep chord in my heart, and I became so emotional, that I had to pull off the road. I got out of the car and knelt down on the side of the highway. Passing motorists must have thought I was out of my mind, but I didn't care. I made a commitment that day to the Lord. I accepted His offer of heaven's dream. I promised that if He only gave me fifty people to pastor for the rest of my life, I would do my best to make them the best-cared-for and best-taught fifty congregants in the world. I promised the Lord that I would never go back to Egypt—meaning Las Vegas. I was here to stay in Fort Lauderdale. This would be my home, and these would be my people. I gave up my former sense of identity and accepted the position of serving God in whatever He called me to do.

> We can't embrace and experience heaven's dreams for us if we're not willing to let go of the familiar.

I was content to be the caretaker of a small group of believers rather than the pastor of a larger church if that was what God had for me.

The next week the church began to grow, and it hasn't stopped since. The Lord has continued to bring people—so many that we've outgrown six locations, including our current one.

What if I had gone back to Las Vegas? I certainly could have, but I would have missed the miracle of having God's fingerprints on my life. Or think of how many people might not have heard the Word of God in a life-changing way if Chuck Smith had never accepted God's challenge to love the hippies back in the 1960s. Out of that first Calvary Chapel, more than a thousand churches have been born, including the one in Fort Lauderdale. Yet because the work is of God, in and through the men and women involved, the ministry will continue long after we are gone.

With eternity in the balance, why do we set up a scale and try to weigh whether it's worth giving up our own pitiful dreams in favor of God's grand dreams for us? It is not advantageous for us to continue playing this game with God. He's not our poker partner. He is our Master, our Lord, and our Creator. He's the one and only eternal God with an eternal perspective and purpose. He is good; He is great; and He is gracious. So why do we hesitate? Could it be the "unknown" factor?

A Venture of Faith

The Bible tells us, "Faith is the substance of things hoped for, the evidence of things not seen" (Hebrews 11:1). How will we ever experience faith if we never venture out from the predictable and the known? When our lives are measured and meted out in a "legal pad" format, with neatly drawn columns that set forth all the details, we leave no room for faith. Some defining aspect of faith must be evident for what happens in our lives to qualify as a true movement of God. God is spirit, and many of the great lessons He teaches us are going to transcend this life's logic. They are lessons of experience that move us closer to attaining the goal of our dreams. We may experience fret and fear, worry and concern as we follow the path of trusting God. But in hindsight we'll discover that these negative emotions constitute the black backdrop against which shines the brilliant diamond of faith.

I counseled a young woman who wanted to learn the lessons of independence without actually separating from her parents. I told her, "You can't." That's like wanting to experience going to an out-of-state college by going to a college in state. It's not possible. By virtue of wanting to go to college out of state, we indicate that we want to learn certain lessons and experience life in a specific way that's conducive to our growth as individuals. That cannot happen in an environment that doesn't provide those opportunities.

We can't embrace and experience heaven's dreams for us if we're not willing to let go of the familiar, false hopes of our self-driven dreams. We'll be locked forever in a temporal and fleeting pursuit of self-glory that will never bring lasting satisfaction. Only those things done for

God's glory remain eternally. I've discovered that doing things for my own glory does not bring the peace, joy, or sense of significance that working for God's glory brings. In fact, when I've looked for significance and success apart from Christ, I've often found futility and restlessness instead.

I witnessed this phenomenon in the lives of others when I worked for Capitol Records. I saw a sad and disconcerting pattern among people who had reached the top of the charts in their careers. Although they had money, power, and fame, they were miserable, lost, and lonely. They had obtained their self-driven dreams only to realize their vanity.

True significance starts with a relationship with God. We cannot begin to grasp the eternal consequences of our efforts unless we're connected to eternity through God's Spirit. Once we've made the decision to accept God's dreams for our lives, He will come to reside in us through His Spirit. His Spirit in us is the means by which He leads and guides us. God's Spirit can be quiet, reserved, and concealed, but I've found that the closer we get to Him, the louder and clearer His voice becomes. Conversely, the further away we are, the harder it is to hear Him.

We stay close by keeping in tune with God by reading His Word and through prayer. We drift when we begin to do our own thing again. So if we're seeking our own self-driven dreams and glory, we'll never discover the eternal dreams God has for us that bring significance and satisfaction. That's why it's critical to determine right from the start whether we're up to the challenge of soul searching.

Are we disillusioned enough with our attempts to find significance, satisfaction, and glory on our own to allow God to do what only He can do? Have we come to the end of our own stabs at making life work? Are we willing to let go of our self-driven dreams and venture out in faith to discover our God-given dreams?

The Call

God has a plan and purpose for each and every individual. That plan cannot even begin, however, until we invite Jesus into our lives. Without the illumination of God's Spirit, we cannot see God's purpose. The apostle Paul wrote that when we accept Christ, we leave darkness and enter the light (see Ephesians 5:8). Light is a physical property that illuminates the definition and clarifies the purpose of an object. We are objects of God's affection, and we have a specific purpose in His plan, but we won't see that until we place ourselves under the light of His Word.

The apostle Peter was so bold that he employed the word *chosen* when referring to those who have come into the family of God through Jesus Christ: "You are a chosen generation, a royal priesthood, a holy nation, His own special people, that you may proclaim the praises of Him who called you out of darkness into His marvelous light" (1 Peter 2:9).

Peter also exhorted us to make our calling and election sure: "Therefore, brethren, be even more diligent to make your call and election sure, for if you do these things you will never stumble" (2 Peter 1:10). Calling is a matter of our service. Election is a matter of our salvation. In God's amazing grace, we have been given light that illuminates our path for salvation, but this same light also leads us to a place of personal fulfillment. This is our calling. We are called to fulfill the dreams God has for us. The Bible tells us that this plan, this dream, was formed before time began:

In Christ, he chose us before the world was made. In his love he chose us to be his holy people—people without blame before him. And before the world was made, God decided to make us his own children through Jesus Christ. That was what he wanted and what pleased him. . . . God has made us what we are. In Christ Jesus, God made us new people so that we would do good works. God had planned in advance those good works for us. He had planned for us to live our lives doing them. (Ephesians 1:4–5; 2:10 ICB)

Sadly, too many of us miss God's dream-illuminating light.

On any given afternoon we can turn on the TV, flip through the channels, and see a circus of characters doing their best to provide entertainment and offer better bodies, romantic getaways, and extreme challenges in sports, games, and survival. There's something for everyone, but as we watch the hundred-plus stations, we're still painfully aware there's nothing on. With all the motion and hype, it is still futility. There's a lot of information, but it's void of inspiration or stimulation to give us a sense of accomplishment, purpose, or reason. After watching, we just feel flat and consumed—certainly not better or wiser.

Herein lies part of the problem: on screen the characters are living out exciting and dramatic lives; but on our side of the screen, we live the same mediocre, monotonous existence day in and day out. Our only drama or excitement comes from what we experience vicariously through the fantasy world of television. The dichotomy between what we perceive to be reality through the lives of those on television and our own boring reality makes us crazy, and we know that somewhere it must end. It does end—in the will of God. There we are given a purpose and a destiny far greater than Indiana Jones had and much more meaningful than a Monday-night football game.

In Luke's Gospel, Jesus exhorts us through a parable, "Do business till I come" (Luke 19:13). If I could take the liberty to paraphrase, Jesus was saying, "Be busy about My business."

Do we grasp the magnitude of the decision we face? We have the opportunity to do God's thing and be blessed beyond our wildest imagination. Or we can continue watching the world pass us by, doing our own mundane thing that ends up leaving us so empty that we settle for vicariously living through someone else.

Arriving at our dreamality will require faith much like that required of the man in Matthew 12: "Jesus said to the man with the crippled hand, 'Let me see your hand.' The man put his hand out, and the hand became well again, the same as the other hand" (Matthew 12:13 ICB).

Jesus asked this man to exercise faith and reach out for what the Lord wanted to give him. The man's response was beautiful. Without excuse or hesitation, he stretched out his hand and was healed. He could have come up with a mountain of reasons why he couldn't stretch out his hand: "What are you, some kind of a wise guy? Can't you see I have a problem with my hand?" Or maybe he could have just stretched out his good hand instead. But he didn't. He knew exactly what Jesus was asking of him. He knew that the moment of truth had come, and he was going to reach out and become what God had designed him to be—a whole man. That's what God does. He makes us whole.

The Challenge

The questions we must answer are, Do we want to be made whole? Do we want the dreams heaven has for us, or are we content to keep chasing our self-driven dreams that can never truly satisfy? If we choose the latter, we'll be fighting against the sovereignty of God. And because He loves us, He won't let us find satisfaction and fulfillment outside of His will for our lives. Each of us was created for a specific reason, and until we discover our signature purpose, we'll spend our lives in vain.

Today I am acting in accordance with a divine script. Even writing this chapter for this book is part and parcel of that divine plan for my life. I'll go even further and say that your reading these words is part of God's divine plan for your life. He is calling you to step into the reality of His dream for you. When we take that step, we'll come to appreciate that nothing we do is outside of God's sovereign control. The apostle Paul put it this way: "In Him we live and move and have our being" (Acts 17:28).

This journey toward realizing heaven's dreams for our lives requires us to be focused on God and not to be found outside of Him. How can we be outside of Him? Those who are outside of God are no longer seeking God's will in their lives but instead are seeking their own way. The writer of Proverbs, King Solomon, understood this. God had given him more wealth and riches than any other king before or after him (see 2 Chronicles 1:11–12), yet Solomon pursued a course of his own. After trying to find satisfaction in this life through these resources, his experience led him to make this astute observation: "The backslider in heart will be filled with his own ways, but a good man will be satisfied from above" (Proverbs 14:14).

We will never discover God's perfect will when we're far away from God, doing our own thing, because at those times we're not even looking for God's will. We will also never be satisfied.

The Bible says, "Ask, and it will be given to you; seek, and you will find; knock, and it will be opened to you. For everyone who asks receives, and he who seeks finds, and to him who knocks it will be opened" (Matthew 7:7–8). Now, if we're not asking, how will we find the answer? If we're not knocking, what door will open? If we're not seeking, how do we think we'll find God?

You are reading for a reason right now. It's your way of asking, seeking, and knocking. God has ordained this opportunity as yet one more chance for you to line up with His will and live the dream He has prepared for you. If you set aside this book and put off discovering His will, you run the risk of never embarking on the journey. If you'll keep reading, I'm confident enough in God's faithfulness to be sure He will give you the answers you've been seeking.

In the next three chapters, we will explore the three components of a God-given dream. Prepare yourself for an adventure that will make all the fantasy of TV pale in comparison.

provision to *share*

Every God-given dream will reflect the benevolence characteristic of our heavenly Father. He lavishes His goodness and resources on us, and when He provides, there's always enough to go around.

In Joseph's dream he saw wheat sheaves, a symbol of provision. The fact that there were multiple sheaves indicated that God desired to provide not just for Joseph's needs but for the needs of others as well. This concept of abundance is seen throughout Scripture and was manifested in Christ's miracle of feeding the five thousand. The underlying principle in all these instances is that God has a heart to bless His people with provision enough to share. He does this so we can experience the blessing of giving that Jesus spoke about: "It is more blessed to give than to receive" (Acts 20:35).

People who have given to others know this truth. They're happier and find more fulfillment in giving than in receiving and keeping wealth for themselves. This is true because we're hard-wired in God's image, and He is the ultimate giver.

God wants to bless us with an abundance divinely determined to be enough to meet our needs and share with others. Our dreams ought to be that we might always be in positions that enable us to share with others so God can be glorified in and through us.

When we give, not only will we be blessed by being used by God, but others will be blessed by having their needs met. When we hoard, only one person's needs are met—yet both the potential giver and the potential recipient end up empty because no matter how much we have, it is never enough. That was the lesson Jesus taught His disciples in the parable of the man who built bigger barns:

> *There was a rich man who had some land, which grew a good crop of food. The rich man thought to himself, "What will I do? I have no place to keep all my crops." Then he said, "I know what I will do. I will tear down my barns and build bigger ones! I will put all my grain and other goods together in my new barns. Then I can say to myself, I have enough good things stored to last for many years. Rest, eat, drink, and enjoy life!"*
>
> *But God said to that man, "Foolish man! Tonight you will die. So who will get those things you have prepared for yourself?"*
>
> *This is how it will be for anyone who stores things up only for himself and is not rich toward God. (Luke 12:16–21 ICB)*

God called this man a fool because he missed the whole point of why God had blessed him in the first place—to share with others.

Co-laboring for God's Glory

Recently I was invited to teach at a Generous Giving conference on the subject of giving and being generous. I found it fascinating that this philanthropic ministry exists to challenge people to be more generous in reaching out to, supporting, and giving to others.

I confronted attendees with this consideration: if you are in a financial or material position of abundance, have you ever considered why you have what you have? The point I went on to make is the same point I'm making here. If we've been successful in our material dreams, it is for a reason that goes beyond the temporal. The Westminster Catechism tells us that the chief end of man is to glorify God and enjoy Him forever.[1] We can do this in a meaningful, powerful way through our finances. As God gifts us, we can be conduits of that prosperity into the lives of others. We can become instruments of and, if I may be so bold, partners with God.

When we see ourselves in the light of eternity as tools in God's hands, we begin to realize part of His amazing dreams for us: that we become co-laborers with Christ to bless the world.

In the book of Exodus, when the people of Israel cried out for deliverance from slavery, God basically told Moses, "I've seen, I'm aware, and I'm sending you." One might ask, why on earth would God use Moses? Why didn't He just do it Himself? I mean, He's God, and He can do anything He wants. He doesn't need us.

That's a valid question I think God is hoping we'll ask, because the answer reveals His fatherly heart toward us.

When my son and I work together on a project, I can do many things for him that I don't. I ask him to do them so he can know the joy of accomplishment, the fellowship of working alongside me, and the satisfaction of having had a hand in the final product. That's the same motivation behind God's using us. He wants us to share in the thrill that comes from doing His work. Giving to and helping others is a spiritual task we accomplish in the physical realm.

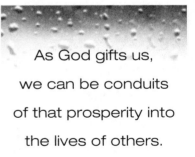

As God gifts us, we can be conduits of that prosperity into the lives of others.

It's the kind of work the book of Ephesians says we were created to do: "We are God's workmanship, created in Christ Jesus to do good works, which God prepared in advance for us to do" (Ephesians 2:10 NIV).

There is, however, a bit of risk involved in being God's partner. It can even get scary. Picture yourself in Moses's shoes at the Red Sea. You've just led over a million people out of Egypt, at the expense of the Egyptians, but you've come to an impassable body of water. When you look back, you see a major dust storm approaching. You look again and realize it's no dust storm; it's the Egyptian army coming after you. Surprise, surprise: Pharaoh has changed his mind *again*. And you know that his son was one of those firstborn killed in the final plague sent by God to secure your release. Now Pharaoh's army is approaching with a blood vendetta, and the gap is closing quickly.

The Bible indicates that the Israelites began to panic. Moses commanded them to be still and watch what God would do: "Do not be afraid. Stand still, and see the salvation of the LORD, which He will accomplish for you today. For the Egyptians whom you see today, you shall see again no more forever. The LORD will fight for you, and you shall hold your peace" (Exodus 14:13–14).

But then the story goes behind the scenes, and if we look closely, we'll catch an inside glimpse of this man of great faith: "The LORD said to Moses, 'Why do you cry to Me? Tell the children of Israel to go forward'" (Exodus 14:15).

In verses 13–14 Moses was speaking to the people. Then suddenly in verse 15 God was answering Moses. Something took place between verses 14 and 15 that might have gone something like this: After boldly telling the people that God would fight for them, Moses cringed privately and began to cry, "Oh God, Oh God, Oh God. We're in trouble now. I told the people to have faith and not to be afraid, but I don't know how You're going to get us out of this one. I sure hope You know what You are doing! I knew this wouldn't work. What are we going to do now? Look at that army. It's huge, horrible, and in a hurry to hack us to pieces. We're between a rock and a hard place. What are You going to do?"

I've taken some liberty with my imagination, but I don't think it's too much, because look at God's response to Moses: "Why do you cry to Me?" Moses may have boldly proclaimed God's imminent deliverance to the Israelites, but to God he showed his true colors.

At this point we have to recognize the magnitude of God's patience with us. Instead of disqualifying Moses for the assignment because he started to falter in his faith, God encouraged him to do something: "Lift up your rod, and stretch out your hand over the sea and divide it. And the children of Israel shall go on dry ground through the midst of the sea" (Exodus 14:16).

Can you imagine Moses's reaction when he lifted his staff and saw the water part?

He led the troops on dry ground until they reached the other side. Pharaoh's soldiers tried to follow, but they were swallowed up when God drowned them in the Red Sea.

If we put ourselves in Moses's shoes, we would be standing in awe at the holy privilege of being used by God. And that is precisely where God wants to put us today—standing in awe at the privilege of *our* being instruments in God's hands.

Losing Our Lives in God

Granted, Moses had enough faith to assure the Israelites they would be safe. Then God granted him faith to see the job through. Notice, however, that Moses had to be willing to step out in that faith. He couldn't be hanging on to his own ways, concerned about what others might think if he lifted his staff and it didn't work. Our co-laboring with God only succeeds when we regard our lives and reputations as expendable items, like Moses did. We have to be willing to let go of our own agendas, including our self-driven dreams, in order to find abundant life—the life that has enough to share. If we don't let go of our own lives, we'll miss our shot at God's life. That's why Jesus said, "He who finds his life will lose it, and he who loses his life for My sake will find it" (Matthew 10:39).

If anyone should know about losing His life, it would be Jesus. That's what He did on the cross. Every drop of blood that was shed at Calvary was an act of God in human flesh laying down, offering, giving His life. He knew that His bloodshed meant redemption, rescue, and freedom for everyone else. It was the joy that was set before Him that enabled Him to endure the cross: "Let us fix our eyes on Jesus, the author and perfecter of our faith, who for the joy set before him endured the cross, scorning its shame, and sat down at the right hand of the throne of God" (Hebrews 12:2 NIV).

If we want to embrace the fullness of the life God has for us, we cannot hold back any part of our lives. The exchange must be complete, and the evidence of that transaction's taking its full course is seen in the sensitive area of giving. Only when we love God with all our hearts, minds, souls, and strength can He infuse us with what we need to be able to share what we have with other people.

Assessing Our Stewardship

The apostle Paul gave an interesting instruction regarding wealth in 1 Timothy 6:17–19: "Command those who are rich in this present age not to be haughty, nor to trust in uncertain riches but in the living God, who gives us richly all things to enjoy. Let them do good, that they be rich in good works, ready to give, willing to share, storing up for themselves a good foundation for the time to come, that they may lay hold on eternal life."

Until our lives are in God alone, we'll tend to trust in our resources rather than in our Redeemer. As long as our finances are our source of security, we won't be able to give freely to others. Instead, we'll hoard our resources in order to feel safe and secure. America is a prime example of this breakdown in our responsibility for spiritual stewardship of what God has given us.

The United States is the richest nation in the world by far. What do we do with our wealth? Records show that in a year's time, we in America have been known to spend:

- $110 billion on fast food
- $85 billion on lawns and gardens
- $64 billion on soft drinks
- $38 billion on state lotteries
- $36 billion on vending-machine products
- $24 billion on jewelry
- $23 billion on toys
- $20 billion on cosmetics
- $13 billion on chocolate
- $7.1 billion on greeting cards
- $600 million on teeth-whitening products[2]

Consider these startling amounts, in light of a few random bits of information, on what it costs to support life in another country:

- Just under $20 will feed a family of four for four weeks in Iraq.[3]
- For $800 you can build a house in Nicaragua, and $25 will feed a family of four for a month.[4]

In light of the immense wealth and prosperity of our nation, Americans are in the best position of all to be generous. We have sufficiently abundant resources to change the face of the world if we take seriously God's desire to work through us in this way. Instead, too many of us are given to gluttony, turn a blind eye to poverty, and continue to chase elusive, self-driven dreams of satisfaction through worldly gain. It won't work. If wealth alone could make us happy, the wealthiest people in the world should be the most content. Yet John D. Rockefeller, one of the richest men in the world, said, "It is wrong to assume that men of immense wealth are always happy."[5]

The problem with trusting in wealth is that money can't save us from the grave. The Bible says that our lives here are like a vapor that vanishes (see James 4:14). Even a long life usually only amounts to around eighty or ninety years. In comparison with eternity, that's not even a blip on the screen. And we can't take our wealth with us when we die. We don't see a U-Haul behind a hearse. The temporal aspect of our earthly lives gives Christ's words all the more relevance and magnitude: "Do not store up for yourselves treasures on earth, where moth and rust destroy, and where thieves break in and steal. But store up for yourselves treasures in heaven, where moth and rust do not destroy, and where thieves do not break in and steal" (Matthew 6:19–20 NIV).

Witnessing through Giving

God is looking for people who will be givers, not hoarders. It is the heart surrendered to God that can be trusted with the God-given dream that includes enough provision to share.

Many of us have heard of Rick Warren, whose book *The Purpose-Driven Life* has sold more than sixteen million copies. What people may not know is what Rick did with his share of the proceeds from those sales. Instead of hoarding the profits, he used the excess to start a ministry called PEACE.[6] This organization has the potential to change how the church does missions.

God gave Rick Warren a dream: to see the church of Jesus Christ recognize the purpose for which it was created. Rick was faithful in relation to that dream (he wrote *The Purpose-Driven Life*), and now God has given him another dream—to see the world won to Christ.

The more we give away, the more God will give to us, because He loves a cheerful giver through whom He can send blessings to the rest of the world. We can become vessels through which God can make

Himself real to others: "We are therefore Christ's ambassadors, as though God were making his appeal through us. We implore you on Christ's behalf: Be reconciled to God" (2 Corinthians 5:20 NIV).

God wants to use our generosity to win the world to Himself. When others see that our security is not in our wealth and that we're willing to give with no strings attached, it's a major witness to the truth of our faith.

A God-given dream will always yield enough to share. That's why God will first challenge our hearts as dream seekers to see if we'll lay down our own dreams and become conduits for God's dream. Will we trust in the Giver rather than in the gift? Are we willing to set a goal to determine how much is enough for ourselves so that when God pours out His abundance, we in turn faithfully share with others?

We could never, even with all our earthly wisdom, develop a business strategy that comes close to what God can accomplish when we simply surrender our hearts and checkbooks to Him. God not only takes care of all our needs, He also graciously allows us to be part of His glorious goodness to others because there is purpose in His provision. It's a means to a higher goal. As Winston Churchill said, "We make a living by what we get. We make a life by what we give."[7]

Giving More Than Money

Think with me for a moment from an eternal perspective in this realm of giving. If, in fact, we are going to spend eternity in heaven, wouldn't it be much wiser to store up treasures there rather than here? This is why we share. We share for the joy of it, for the participation in it, and for the satisfaction of accomplishing something of eternal value.

That's why God's provision for us to share doesn't just include material wealth. It includes all we do and all we are. God provides for us in every area of our human existence—material, emotional, intellectual, and spiritual—and He grants us more than we need for the benefit of others.

Emotional Giving

We live in a world of ever-increasing emotional isolation. From fences between neighbors to separate bedrooms for husbands and wives, we are experiencing a breakdown in our ability to share our lives with others. How many people are willing to just cry with someone, or let someone cry with them? How do we respond when someone breaks down emotionally? As a society we are drifting further and further apart emotionally. Our friendships, too, often lack depth because we insist on being superficial. It's all about fun and good times, but that's not life. Life includes times that are neither fun nor good. And it's in those times of disappointment, doubt, discouragement, and downright ugliness that true bonding occurs. Yet we've become so guarded that we don't let anyone know when we're hurting. We don't want to bear the burden of the unpleasant details of our friends' trials, so we figure they don't want to bear the burden of ours either. That's unfortunate, because this realm of open and transparent communication is where true friendship flourishes.

William H. Terry, in his sermon "Virtues for Living," said: "I read once of two ladies who sold flowers in the Charleston market. For years they had occupied adjoining stalls. One day a customer noticed that one [of] the stalls was vacant and asked the other flower lady where her neighbor was. She had died. The customer said, 'Oh! That must have made you very sad. You were such friends.' 'No'm,' she replied, 'We weren't really friends. We never cried together.'"[8] Those women had known each other but had never had the emotional exchange that bonds us as human beings.

Friendships are made and kept by sharing life's joys and pains, enjoying each other's strengths while putting up with each other's imperfections, and extending lots of love and forgiveness. Friendships are made by sharing each other's dreams and dreads, truths and consequences, pleasures and sorrows.

When God gives a dream, with that dream will come the provision to share in more than just the financial arena. In our lives are people with whom God desires that we share the emotional strength He has given us. The Bible says, "Praise be to the God and Father of our Lord Jesus Christ, the Father of compassion and the God of all comfort, who comforts us in all our troubles, so that we can comfort those in any trouble with the comfort we ourselves have received from God. For just as the sufferings of Christ flow over into our lives, so also through Christ our comfort overflows" (2 Corinthians 1:3–5 NIV).

Intellectual Giving

Sometimes the gift we can share is neither financial nor emotional but intellectual. Proverbs 27:17 says, "As iron sharpens iron, so one man sharpens another" (NIV). We have the ability to spur one another on in the arena of our thoughts.

When I was working with my writing team on this chapter, we found ourselves getting excited about sharing ideas, stopping at certain points and saying, "Oh, there's a great verse that would fit right here." This mental exchange is something God intended to be a positive and stimulating component of the human experience. Too many people today are so overloaded and stressed that their conversations are more aggravating than exhilarating. God inspires us with thoughts, and He wants us to share the revelations He gives us with others to help them in their own situations.

I was recently on a radio program with Justin Alfred, who is a brilliant Bible scholar. Afterward I asked him to stay on the line with me for a while privately. I figured I had an opportunity I don't often get, and I wanted to pick his brain. As we spoke, just the two of us, I said, "Justin, I have a question for you. The brazen laver—what did they use it for?" Now I realize that only Bible enthusiasts would get excited over the brazen laver, but that's not the point. The point is that as we began to kick around a few ideas together, iron was sharpening iron.

I shared with him my experience in Israel of seeing the troughs that people in Bible times would walk into for a cleansing experience. When they came out, a priest would be standing by to pronounce them clean or unclean. This was a powerful experience for them, and the brazen laver was a part of it. I expressed to Justin that I thought there might have been in the brazen laver an extra act of ceremonial washing that made them clean.

As the conversation progressed, I was tying that ritual together with water baptism because in water baptism God declares us clean. Our discussion went a little further, and I mentioned the sheet that came down from heaven for the apostle Peter in Acts 10, when God told him not to call anything unclean that He had made clean. Then Justin said, "Do you want to go back a little further? Remember, John's baptism was a baptism of repentance. When he began to preach a baptism of repentance, people already had an understanding that they needed to go into the water and be submerged and then come back up again." As we bounced one thought after another off each other, we came to some inspiring and profound truths that I don't think I would have thought of on my own.

> Christianity is not a religion for the mindless. It is not a faith without facts.

I don't know what stimulates you intellectually—probably not the brazen laver—but the purpose of my example is to show you how, within just a few minutes of conversation, our minds were ablaze with thoughts and ideas. Because Justin and I walk in our God-given dreams, we have enough provision to share with one another intellectually.

Christianity is not a religion for the mindless. It is not a faith without facts. Yet I did not discover many of these facts until I was ready to step out in faith and walk in the life God had for me. Once I did that, I found out some fascinating things that convinced me intellectually that God, whom I cannot see, is more real than all that I can see.

The Bible affirms that as Christians, "we have the mind of Christ" (1 Corinthians 2:16). That means that we, above all other human beings, should be creative, inspired, intelligent, and wise. God gives us the mind of Christ so we can share with others in this important arena of the mind.

In Malachi 3:16–18 the Bible records a fascinating fact:

Those who honored the Lord spoke with each other. The Lord listened and heard them. The names of those who honored the Lord and respected him were written in a book. The Lord will remember them.

The Lord of heaven's armies says, "They belong to me. On that day they will be my very own. A father shows mercy to his son who serves him. In the same way I will show mercy to my people. You will again see the difference between good and evil people. You will see the difference between those who serve God and those who don't."[3] *(ICB)*

When we do this intellectual sparring with one another over spiritual things, God is listening. Even more amazing is that based on what we say, God is determining whether we belong to Him. These types of dialogue will also be evidence to others that we are good people rather than evil ones, and that we serve God, because we intellectually acknowledge Him in our conversations.

Spiritual Giving

Although the influence of our lives on the world around us would be profound if we were to take seriously the lesson about blessing others financially, emotionally, and intellectually, the greatest impact we can have on our world as a result of our God-given dreams is spiritual.

When we make that all-consuming decision to let go of our self-driven dreams in exchange for heaven's dreams, we step out of the temporal realm in which we've existed thus far into the spiritual realm where God lives. This is not just a matter of adding God to our lives; it is a far greater transition. God actually becomes our life. Look at how the Bible describes this change:

- *"You were once darkness, but now you are light in the Lord. Walk as children of light." (Ephesians 5:8)*

- *"In the past all of us lived like them. We lived trying to please our sinful selves. We did all the things our bodies and minds wanted. We should have suffered God's anger because of the way we were. We were the same as all other people.*

   "But God's mercy is great, and he loved us very much. We were spiritually dead because of the things we did wrong against God. But God gave us new life with Christ. You have been saved by God's grace. And he raised us up with Christ and gave us a seat with him in the heavens. He did this for those of us who are in Christ Jesus." (Ephesians 2:3–6 ICB)

- *"I have been crucified with Christ and I no longer live, but Christ lives in me. The life I live in the body, I live by faith in the Son of God, who loved me and gave himself for me. I do not set aside the grace of God, for if righteousness could be gained through the law, Christ died for nothing!" (Galatians 2:20–21 NIV)*

- *"We did not receive the spirit of the world, but we received the Spirit that is from God. We received this Spirit so that we can know all that God has given us." (1 Corinthians 2:12 ICB)*

When we walk in heaven's dreams for our lives, we are spiritually connected and in tune with the Almighty Himself. This connection is critical in our world today. A search for the word *spiritual* on Google will result in more than twenty million listings. Our world is spiritually hungry! And with our God-given dreams comes spiritual food enough to feed the multitudes.

Understanding That We're Designed to Give

Sharing is not natural. It takes divine intervention. I haven't had to teach my kids to say "mine." It was something they knew from the start. Selfishness is part of fallen, sinful human nature. Yet if the human spirit does not share, it will die, because we were originally created in the image of God, who is a giver. Jesus said it's more blessed to give than to receive because He knew that giving is part of the healthy life God designed us to have.

Giving is a spiritual exercise that moves us away from the flesh, which brings only death and destruction. The joy we get from sharing is designed to combat anything that would hold us back from giving to others. It takes us out of the realm of the natural and taps into the eternal. This joy reaches to the very core of who we are and resonates with the inner sense we have of being part of something bigger than ourselves. If we hang on to our self-driven dreams, we will never discover this supernatural realm.

Giving with Purpose

When we truly comprehend that our abundance—whether material, emotional, intellectual, spiritual, or some other category of human experience—is meant to bless others, we feel an excitement and anticipation in every moment of our day. We know God has something someone else needs, and we want Him to give it to us so we can give it to that person. We become agents of eternity, reminiscent of the old TV program *The Millionaire*, in which a representative of a wealthy philanthropic donor would seek out an unsuspecting person to be the recipient of a million dollars. The show would then tell the story of the person's life and how the gift impacted him or her. In much the same way, we're on a quest to give away God's fortune to those less fortunate people in our world, and we're privileged to be included in the blessing that brings.

Even at the tender age of seven, my son caught on to this principle of being others-centered. We went to McDonald's because the Happy Meal prize was supposed to be a Disney princess. Christian was excited for his sister, Caitlyn, because she loves everything princess. The kids got their Happy Meals and opened them up only to discover Bratz dolls. Caitlyn was disappointed and didn't want the doll. Two nights later, right after we finished dinner, Christian said, "Hey, Dad, Mom loves hot-fudge sundaes from McDonald's, and I think they have the princess gifts now. Maybe we could go there for dessert."

"I don't know, Son," I said. "We just finished our meal."

"Dad, you know I have some allowance money. I know we just ate, but could I buy Cait just the prize so she could have a princess toy? I would pay for it out of my allowance."

You can imagine the joy in my heart when I heard my child saying he was willing to give away something of his for the sake of someone else. God must feel the same way when He sees His children give to others. That's the spirit God is looking for. He wants someone who is willing to give sacrificially for the sake of another, following the example Jesus set for us on the cross.

In our lives there is no greater expression of who God is than for us to be willing to give to others, because God is the ultimate Giver. To be given resources by God and to not give them away is like keeping a Ferrari in idle. How long can we live like that? If we don't give, we'll implode or explode. Our hospitals and psychiatrists' offices are full of people doing just that.

Our world is starving, and we have God's provision. When we step out in faith and accept the challenge to share, God opens the door and reveals the second aspect of our God-given dream—the power to save.

power to *save*

Although God's dreams for us include sufficient provision to share with others, we can't give away what we don't have. That's why at this juncture of our journeys toward fulfilling God's dreams for our lives, we must stop and get our bearings for the remainder of the trip. Many of us have lost our dreams somewhere along the way, and in a sense, God has lost His dream as well. It happened back in the Garden of Eden with the fall of Adam and Eve, when humanity became separated from fellowship with the Creator.

This is why God wants so much to give us back our dreams. When we get our dreams back, He gets His dream back, because the dreams He has for us bring us back into the purpose for which we were created—to have fellowship with and glorify Him. This common link between God's own dream and His dreams for us embodies the vital dynamic of power to save that is inherent in every God-given dream.

The Necessity of Salvation

The dictionary defines *salvation* as "the preservation or deliverance from destruction, difficulty, or evil."[1] To see how this ability to save manifests itself through heaven's dreams for us, we need to look at what we are being saved from.

Contrary to common belief, God does not save us from hell. The salvation He provides is much greater than that. God saves us from sin. Hell is simply one of the consequences of sin. Those who die without being saved from sin go to hell. Those who die, having been saved from sin, go to heaven. The Bible says, "Whoever has the Son has life. But the person who does not have the Son of God does not have life" (1 John 5:12 ICB).

The power to save is found in Christ alone because He is the salvation of mankind: "Jesus is the only One who can save people. His name is the only power in the world that has been given to save people. And we must be saved through him!" (Acts 4:12 ICB). This verse may seem narrow-minded until we understand why it's true. To comprehend the reasoning behind Christ's unique position to save, it's necessary to consider heaven's dream and to discover how it was lost and why sin has to be dealt with before either God or we can get our dreams back.

Heaven's Dream Destroyed

God's dream was for mankind to enjoy unbroken fellowship with Him for all eternity. God is life, and death was never part of His original plan. Death entered the world as a result of sin: "Sin came into the world because of what one man did. And with sin came death" (Romans 5:12 ICB). Before we can grasp the impact Adam and Eve's sin had on humanity, let me paint a backdrop against which this powerful point can be seen more clearly.

One of the attributes ascribed to God in Scripture is that He is self-existent (see Psalms 90:2; 115:3; Isaiah 43:10–13; 57:15; Jeremiah 23:23–24; John 5:26; Romans 11:34–36). This means that God is outside time and space, has no beginning or end, and requires no one or nothing outside Himself to exist. Yet God, in His self-sufficiency, chose to create humans to be the objects of His affection. He created us for fellowship with Him in order that He might lavish upon us a love so divine and rich that it had to be shared.

Most of us know the story of Adam and Eve in the Garden of Eden. What some may not know about this story is the depth of disappointment that single act of disobedience brought to the heart of God—not because He's a tyrant who demands absolute obedience, as some think, but because He is a loving Creator and Father who knew the consequences sin would bring. He had warned Adam and Eve that eating of the tree of the knowledge of good and evil would bring death, but they didn't heed His warning. As a result they experienced death.

We tend to think of death as the point when we cease to exist, but this isn't really an accurate definition. The truth is that we all will live eternally. Death, then, is not an end to existence but rather a separation: When we die physically, our souls separate from our bodies. When we die emotionally, our intellect disconnects from our feelings. When we die spiritually, we are separated from God. That's what happened to Adam and Eve, and it has been happening to all of us ever since. When God said that Adam and Eve would die if they ate the fruit of that tree, He was telling them the truth. The manifestation of that experience was felt first spiritually, but eventually emotionally, and finally physically.

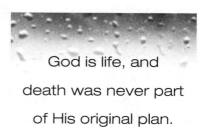

God is life, and death was never part of His original plan.

Adam and Eve's sin left them disconnected from God, who is the source of all life and goodness. That separation ultimately led to death and destruction in every area of their existence. This slow-but-sure death is similar to what happens to a branch when it has been cut off from a tree. For a while the disconnected branch will still have the appearance of being alive, but because it cannot drink from the source that once gave it life, it will eventually die.

Death became the legacy Adam and Eve passed on to mankind. It wasn't our choice, but neither was it my choice to have hazel eyes. I have hazel eyes because of the genes passed on to me by my parents. Likewise, we have a sinful nature because the parents of the human race passed it on to us. And with that also came the heartbreaking reality that all of mankind has been separated from God.

God's dream of unbroken fellowship with His creation was lost when Adam and Eve believed the lie of Satan over the truth of God. God had offered limitless provision for this couple. It was as though God had a store in which they could choose whatever they wanted—except for one thing. God's shelves are stocked with everything that makes life good, transforming, and redeeming. But Satan has a storehouse too, and his is filled with lies. Jesus called him the father of lies (see John 8:44). Satan's shelves are full of everything that kills, robs, steals, and destroys (see John 10:10). All he has to offer is from his own inventory.

Like Adam and Eve, we make our choices—either from the devil's store of lies or from God's store of blessing—and so determine the courses of our lives. We can keep shopping in the devil's store, buying the same lie that brought death to Adam and Eve, and reap the same deadly consequences. Or we can go to God's store instead and find everything we need for a fulfilling life.

Unfortunately for all of us, Adam and Eve bought the devil's lie that they would be like God if they ate from the tree. We'll look at Satan's strategy in greater detail later on, since he is a major opponent in our quest to discover God's dreams for our lives. But now let's examine an interesting point about the lie he told Adam and Eve.

Like most of Satan's lies, this one was laced with an element of truth. Otherwise. they probably never would have bought it. As the serpent promised, Adam and Eve would know good and evil after they ate the fruit. But Satan didn't tell them the whole truth. Adam and Eve already knew good. Everything God had given them was good. That means all they got from obeying Satan rather than God was the knowledge of evil.

Satan also failed to tell them that although they would be able to know good and evil like God, they would not have the power to choose good over evil. Their act of disobedience would separate them from God, who alone has the power to overcome evil. It was the original bait and switch. The devil's temptation held out the hope that in eating the fruit, Adam and Eve would become more like God in their ability to have knowledge. As promised, like God, they could see their sinfulness; but unlike God, there was nothing they could do about it. What they actually got was the ability to know just how hideous their choice had been.

The Problem of Sin

Why couldn't God just overlook the sin? He's God, isn't He, and He loves us, doesn't He?

Yes, He is God, and He does love us, which is why He couldn't just overlook Adam and Eve's sin. As we'll see later in this chapter, to overlook sin would have been the most unloving thing God could have done. We would have been left for all eternity in a state of separation from God, in the grip of sin, and on course for destruction.

God had to deal with the sin, for His sake and ours. The Bible clearly states that God is love, but it also explains that sin separates us from God: "Your iniquities have separated you from your God; and your sins have hidden His face from you, so that He will not hear" (Isaiah 59:2). Sin separates us from God because it is in complete opposition to His holiness. For God to join Himself in fellowship with sin would be like us, as human beings, trying to live in a room without oxygen. Even if we wanted to, we couldn't. Whether we love being without air or not isn't the question; it's simply a fact that human life requires oxygen.

Similarly, holiness requires sinlessness. For God to embrace or tolerate sin would, for Him, be less than holy. It cannot and will not happen. The character of God cannot be compromised, because then He would be less than God.

God is also just and righteous. Overlooking sin would make Him unjust and unrighteous. Would we want God to wink His eye at sin when that sin is one of child molestation or brutal torture and murder? No, we want a God who is just when it comes to wrongdoing. Although God is love, He also is just. He cannot compromise one essence for the other and still be God.

The movie *Camelot* offers a beautiful analogy of God's position regarding sin. In many ways the story parallels the biblical account of the Fall. Camelot was a place of peace and prosperity under the rule of King Arthur. Like Eden, however, the innocence of Camelot was lost through unfaithfulness. When Arthur discovered that Guinevere was having an affair with Sir Lancelot, he was torn between his love for Guinevere and his responsibility as king. The law demanded Guinevere's death, but the king could not fathom how he would ever be able to give the order for her execution. His counselors reminded him that the duty of the king is to mete out justice, and to let her go unpunished would call into question his position as king because it would reflect irresponsibility to the authority of that title.

In the Bible God portrays Himself as the husband of His people (see Isaiah 54:5). We, like Guinevere, have been unfaithful. God's justice demands our death. But like King Arthur, whose heart shrunk back from ordering Guinevere's death, God's love keeps Him from abandoning us to destruction.

The Savior

The most amazing facet of this entire scenario, and where the movie parallel departs, is that God, in His omniscience, knew that Adam and

Eve would be unfaithful. Before He ever commanded, "Let there be light" (Genesis 1:3), He knew that His dream would be lost. But He also knew it would not be a permanent loss, because He had a plan. God's justice required punishment for sin—and His love volunteered to take the penalty on our behalf.

This, by the way, was not Plan B. This was God's plan from the beginning. That's why the Bible calls Jesus the Lamb that was slain from the foundation of the world (see Revelation 13:8).

Forgive me if you've already connected the dots, but let me point out the implications here: all-sufficient, self-existing, almighty God, who has no need of anyone or anything, loves us so much that He was willing to take the penalty of our sin so we can return to the original purpose for which He created us—to have fellowship with Him. The Bible tells us that this is the reason God sent His Son, Jesus, to die. Follow the progression of events as laid out in these scriptures:

- *"All have sinned and fall short of the glory of God." (Romans 3:23)*

- *"The wages of sin is death, but the gift of God is eternal life in Christ Jesus our Lord." (Romans 6:23)*

- *"God loved the world so much that he gave his only Son. God gave his Son so that whoever believes in him may not be lost, but have eternal life." (John 3:16 ICB)*

- *"Christ died for us while we were still sinners. In this way God shows his great love for us.*

   "We have been made right with God by the blood of Christ's death. So through Christ we will surely be saved from God's anger. I mean that while we were God's enemies, God made friends with us through the death of his Son. Surely, now that we are God's friends, God will save us through his Son's life. And not only that, but now we are also very happy in God through our Lord Jesus Christ. Through Jesus we are now God's friends again.

"Sin came into the world because of what one man did. And with sin came death. And this is why all men must die—because all men sinned. . . .

"After Adam sinned once, he was judged guilty. But the gift of God is different. God's free gift came after many sins. And the gift makes people right with God. One man sinned, and so death ruled all people because of that one man. But now some people accept God's full grace and the great gift of being made right with him. They will surely have true life and rule through the one man, Jesus Christ.

"So one sin of Adam brought the punishment of death to all people. But in the same way, one good act that Christ did makes all people right with God. And that brings true life for all. One man disobeyed God, and many became sinners. But in the same way, one man obeyed God, and many will be made right." (Romans 5:8–12, 16–19 ICB)

God loves us so much that He wouldn't leave us in our sin. He's so great that He could and did pay the penalty for the wrong we did to Him.

God's tremendous love and sacrifice also demonstrate that He is worthy of our trust because He has our best interest at heart. He's not out to ruin our fun, and His laws are not in place to keep us from enjoying life. On the contrary, He gave us His Word so we can live life to the fullest.

In the Gospel of John, Jesus said, "The thief does not come except to steal, and to kill, and to destroy. I have come that they may have life, and that they may have it more abundantly" (John 10:10). Jesus is the living, breathing, incarnate Word of God, the second person of the triune godhead. He told us that to find true life, we must abide in Him (see John 15:5). The way we abide in Him is through studying the written Word of God. It's in Scripture that we find the incredible story of the love between God and mankind. It's in Scripture that we find amazing examples of people who have realized the goodness of God, accepted heaven's dreams for their lives, and experienced the joy that comes from God's dream: restored fellowship with us. And it is in Scripture that we find the principles that keep us in the love of God, imparting life to us daily as we walk in a world filled with sin and death.

The Accomplishment of Salvation

Now, against this backdrop of God's tremendous plan for salvation, let's consider again the definition of the word *salvation*: "the preservation or deliverance from destruction, difficulty, or evil." God's salvation delivers us from the penalty of sin, which is destruction, difficulty, and evil. But He also preserves us in this life. The salvation God offers is not just for when this life is over; it extends to the here and now as well. Through Jesus we are connected back to the source of life. Jesus called this experience being "born again" (John 3:3). We must be born again because, through Adam and Eve, we all have suffered the death that came from their disobedience: separation from God. In Christ we receive life again—we are reconnected to God, the source of all life. In Him there is no death.

When we accept Christ's offer of atonement for our sins through His death on the cross, we are restored to fellowship with God. It's like going back to the Garden of Eden before the Fall. Through disobedience, Adam and Eve sinned and were separated from God. But through Christ's obedience, the penalty of death has been paid. By accepting Christ's free gift of salvation, we reconnect to Life itself. So death—separation from God—has been overcome by Life—reconnection to God.

Reconnection with God shows itself in every area of our lives. Salvation is a matter of preserving us from some of the effects of sin in this world. Although our physical bodies are subject to death, our reconnection with God preserves our souls from death (see Matthew 10:28). This reconnection to God frees us from bondage to sin (see Romans 6:7) and allows us to live lives that reflect our freedom in the choices we make.

Without even considering the eternal benefits of a life that chooses righteousness over sin, we reap an almost instant benefit in this life. When I came to Christ, I no longer indulged in physically damaging behavior that had been part of my lifestyle up until that point. God only knows how many years have been added to my life here and now because I no longer abuse massive amounts of cocaine, alcohol, and other drugs. I treat women with respect rather than using them. Salvation has given me more than just life after death. It has given me a longer, healthier, and more productive life for the duration of my time on earth. And the choices I make because I'm saved positively affect all my other relationships. How I handle my finances, how I raise my kids, how I treat others in my business dealings, and how I conduct myself in every other area reflects the fact that I am now connected to a holy and righteous God.

Salvation is a pervasive process that manifests itself in and through us and glorifies God in the process. Those who knew me before I was saved can see the marked difference in every area of my life. My family and close friends know that I would never have been able to do what God has done in my life, so they are left with no alternative but to give God the credit.

Salvation, then, is how God gets His dream back. His dream is that we will walk in the glory for which He created us. We are meant for greatness because we're created in the image of a great and mighty God. But if we don't experience God's power to save, we stay trapped in our mediocre, lifeless, and pointless existences.

My son has action figures called Transformers. Each toy can actually be two different things: a robot that has special abilities to fight and win battles, or a vehicle, like a car, truck, or plane. But imagine a Transformer that never gets transformed, that always stays a truck. That's what we're like when we never experience the transforming power of God's salvation. We never discover the other part of who we are—who we were meant to be in Christ. In the nature we inherited from Adam, we only know what a human being, limited by the handicap of sin, can do. We haven't been transformed so we can soar, accomplish great things, and win spiritual battles. How mediocre, empty, and futile this life is without heaven's dream of more.

Millions of people live in this mundane condition. They settle for being just a car, plane, or truck. The saddest part is that all the while, their spirits are crying out for transformation. In our hearts, we know we were created for glory, not for the dull disillusionment we too often accept.

The Bible says, "God decided to let his people know this rich and glorious truth which he has for all people. This truth is Christ himself, who is in you. He is our only hope for glory" (Colossians 1:27 ICB). If you have yet to be transformed, grab hold of this truth in your own life. Allow God to reconnect you to Himself through Christ's work of restoration on the cross.

The Burden of Sin

Without God we are doomed to a hopeless, helpless existence that has no purpose, and we're also doomed to the consequences of sin. We tend to think of sin as those horrific crimes people commit, like murder, theft, child abuse, incest, torture, and other heinous acts of depravity members of the human race perpetrate on one another. Horrors such as the Holocaust stand as indictments against the false theory of mankind's goodness and as confirmation of the Bible's position that we're all sinners. Human history is full of reminders of just how evil we can be.

Most of us, however, are so far removed from tragedies like the Holocaust that we don't relate them to the sinful condition of our own hearts. But Jesus closed the comfortable gap between such terrible sins and our own with this statement: "You have heard that it was said to our people long ago, 'You must not murder anyone. Anyone who murders another will be judged.' But I tell you, if you are angry with your brother, you will be judged. And if you say bad things to your brother, you will be judged by the Jewish council. And if you call your brother a fool, then you will be in danger of the fire of hell" (Matthew 5:21–22 ICB).

As we saw in chapter 1, when we looked at Luke's parable about giving good gifts to our kids (Luke 11:11–13), and in our discussion of Adam and Eve's sin earlier in this chapter, mankind is inherently evil because we have been infected with sin as a result of the Fall. This sinful condition causes us to be self-centered and ultimately capable of every wicked act. The Holocaust happened because of the unchecked sin of hatred. The Bible teaches that all sin starts in the human heart: "Do you know where your fights and arguments come from? They come from the selfish desires that make war inside you. You want things, but you do not have them. So you are ready to kill and are jealous of other people. But you still cannot get what you want. So you argue and fight. You do not get what you want because you do not ask God" (James 4:1–2 ICB).

These verses describe the heart of a person who has not asked for God's salvation. The Bible says that we are all in need of the Savior (see Isaiah 53; Romans 3:23; Acts 4:12). We may not be Hitlers, but without the transformation brought by the finished work of Christ's atoning death, we are capable of every sin known to mankind. From the unkind words we speak to our spouses to the little white lies we tell our employers or the IRS, we are sowing the seeds of sin that bring forth death.

The lie we continue to buy from the devil's store is that if we can get away with it, it doesn't matter or count. As sincerely as we may believe this, it's not true. The Word of God says, "Do not be deceived: God cannot be mocked. A man reaps what he sows. The one who sows to please his sinful nature, from that nature will reap destruction; the one who sows to please the Spirit, from the Spirit will reap eternal life" (Galatians 6:7–8 NIV). Even though we may get away with sin for the moment, the consequences will come. Our guilt festers, and our sinful actions will have repercussions, whether in the breakdown of a relationship, the breakdown of our mental or physical well-being, or, in the worst-case scenario, a breakdown before the judgment seat of God.

Guilt is a merciless master that never lets up. It's a dream destroyer because it keeps us in touch with our unworthiness.

I was fascinated to hear accounts of people who, after seeing Mel Gibson's film *The Passion of the Christ*, confessed to crimes they had committed and had "gotten away with." Although they had been able to escape the outward penalty for their actions, sin still took its toll.

Guilt is a merciless master that never lets up. It's a dream destroyer because it keeps us in touch with our unworthiness. Some people give in to guilt and give up their dreams. Others fight to prove that they're worth something after all. That's how some self-driven dreams arise. In an effort to make something of ourselves apart from God, we forfeit family, friends, and even sanity. We're desperate to escape the guilt that tells us we're not worthy of the glorious life we desire from the deepest part of ourselves.

One of the more profound aspects of my own conversion to Christ was the removal of the burden of guilt and the realization that my worth stems from God's evaluation of me, not my own or anyone else's. As a pastor who hears many testimonies, I've noticed that this release from guilt is a common denominator.

No other religion offers a real solution to guilt. From the humanistic mind-set that it's someone else's fault, to the Buddhist theory that guilt doesn't really exist because there is no right or wrong, to any other theory out there, we find no relief from the nagging reminder that something is radically wrong. We have fallen from the glory for which we were intended, and our souls, which are eternal, know this. That fallen nature might manifest itself in lying, cheating, adultery, fornication, or any of an endless list of symptoms that indicate we're still under the stranglehold of sin, but the underlying cause in each instance is the loss of our connection with the Source of life. Because of that, we are walking in death.

The Gift of Grace

Considering the incredible burden of sin, one might think everyone would be flocking to Jesus. Not so. We're so bound and blinded by sin that we just can't believe the solution is so simple. We've been taught that if we're going to get anything out of this life, we have to work for it. We've learned well that nothing in life is free, and if we want to survive and be successful, we'd better go further and do better than the next person. We've become so wise in our own eyes that we consider the message of the Cross to be foolishness.

God knew this would be the case. Paul wrote, "The teaching about the cross seems foolish to those who are lost. But to us who are being saved it is the power of God. . . . The world did not know God through its own wisdom. So God chose to use the message that sounds foolish to save those who believe it" (1 Corinthians 1:18, 21 ICB).

God also knew it would take humility to admit that we're unable to deal with the effects of sin on our own and that we would need a savior. Only in humility and simplicity can a heart embrace the power of the Cross that brings salvation from sin, reconnection to God, and a release from guilt, because only in humility do we find the power from God to do so: "'God resists the proud, but gives grace to the humble'" (1 Peter 5:5). It is "by grace you have been saved through faith, and that not of yourselves; it is the gift of God, not of works, lest anyone should boast" (Ephesians 2:8–9). Humility opens the door for God to give the grace by which we are saved from sin and relieved of guilt.

As we look again at the life of Joseph, we see that he did not abandon his dream, but neither did he pursue his own course of action to make the dream come true. Even after his brothers tried to kill him and then sold him into slavery, even after he was falsely accused by his master's wife and wound up in prison, Joseph never gave up on God. We see this in his interaction with two other prisoners who had fallen into disfavor with Pharaoh:

> *It came to pass after these things that the butler and the baker of the king of Egypt offended their lord, the king of Egypt. And Pharaoh was angry with his two officers, the chief butler and the chief baker. So he put them in custody in the house of the captain of the guard, in the prison, the place where Joseph was confined. And the captain of the guard charged Joseph with them, and he served them; so they were in custody for a while.*
>
> *Then the butler and the baker of the king of Egypt, who were confined in the prison, had a dream, both of them, each man's dream in one night and each man's dream with its own interpretation. And Joseph came in to them in the morning and looked at them, and saw that they were sad. So he asked Pharaoh's officers who were with him in the custody of his lord's house, saying, "Why do you look so sad today?"*
>
> *And they said to him, "We each have had a dream, and there is no interpreter of it."*
>
> *So Joseph said to them, "Do not interpretations belong to God? Tell them to me, please." (Genesis 40:1–8)*

Had Joseph become bitter and turned his back on God, his interaction with these men would have been quite different. He might not have even had the inclination to find out why they were so sad. He certainly wouldn't have given God credit for interpretation of dreams, and he wouldn't have made the subsequent request to know the dream, which implies his ongoing relationship with God. Since Joseph established that God gives the interpretation of dreams, it stands to reason that he wouldn't have been so bold to ask about the dreams if he had been disconnected from the source of their interpretation.

This seemingly insignificant encounter speaks volumes about Joseph's relationship with God. Joseph obviously was operating in God's grace, which comes only to the humble, and it is this humility that kept Joseph in right standing with God and ultimately in a position to realize God's dream for his life. And he remained in a position through which God could orchestrate salvation in the lives of others: his family from starvation, but more importantly, the nation of Israel from total destruction and thus elimination of the lineage of the Messiah.

> When we approach life with an attitude of self-centeredness, it's difficult to hear the gentle voice of our Father offering us dreams He has prepared on our behalf.

When we approach life with an attitude of self-centeredness, which is the earmark of a life in bondage to sin, it's difficult to hear the gentle voice of our Father offering us dreams He has prepared on our behalf. As we saw, the Bible says that God resists the proud but gives grace to the humble, and that we are saved through grace. As we put these truths together, we can see more clearly the scheme of the Enemy to keep us bound up in pride so that we become disqualified for the grace that accompanies humility. We must not let Satan use pride to keep us from the gift of grace that has power to save.

The Power of a Transformed Life

Salvation is God's transforming power in the life of everyday people. Listen to the compelling story of one of them:

Childhood is supposed to be a time of carefree activity and unabated innocence, but when that innocence is stripped away, so is the carefree life. In an instant, life becomes pitiful and burdensome, and a child loses his childhood for good. That's what happened to me, and this is my story.

My dad was in the Navy and proud of it. When I was a young kid, my family moved back to upstate New York to be near my father's family. Early on, I felt the ugliness of prejudice and racism. My father is black, and my mother is white—a racial partnership that was not at all accepted in the early sixties.

Yet in my neighborhood, I thrived. I had a friendship with my Grandpa Joe, who paid more attention to me than my own father, and I had a friendship with him that kept me going.

My family went to church because that was what we were supposed to do. My dad wasn't a bad man, but we just didn't have much of a relationship. In fact, from the age of eleven on, we had no relationship at all. This bothered me. Like any other kid, I figured out a way to adjust to the way things were—that is, until the day my cousin molested me, betrayed my trust, and stole my childhood. It's amazing, looking back, how my whole life changed in a flash. He destroyed my identity, took away my sense of self-worth, and introduced me to the perverted world of pornography.

After that, my life began to spiral down with a steady acceleration.

By the age of twelve, I already had a reputation of being a partyer. I began experimenting with sex and would do anything to get a girl's attention. In fact, at one of my first parties, I allowed a girl to pierce my ear just to get her to notice me.

In middle school, I started coming home drunk. I thought I was so cool, and soon I took up smoking pot as well. In my mind, the more I partied, the more I was accepted and liked. I didn't get it that trying to find acceptance would actually end up isolating me and driving me to despair.

By high school, I was addicted to drugs, sex, girls, and pornography. As with any addiction, I needed a stronger and stronger fix to get the same thrills and highs. I graduated from pot to cocaine and then on to crack. Meanwhile my sexual appetite was becoming more and more weird.

By eighteen, I was a full-blown addict. I was also something else—I was ashamed and confused. Though I knew my behavior was wrong, I really didn't know what normal was either. My whole outlook on relationships was messed up, and my sexual desires and relations were perverted.

My parents got fed up with my behavior, and my dad wouldn't have anything to do with me. I thought he was a jerk and wanted my mother to divorce him.

Then something happened to my mom and dad. They found God, and it began to reflect in their attitudes. Instead of fighting, they started to back each other up. There was a spirit of unity in our home that had never been there before. Along with their new partnership came a renewed interest in disciplining their children—something that did not go over well with me.

My life was headed nowhere. I was busy selling drugs on my school campus and had no desire to study or think about getting a job. It was Grandpa Joe that sat me down one day and tried to bring a dose of reality into my life.

He told me I needed to do something with my life and that maybe I should go to automotive tech school since my grades weren't good enough to get me into college, so that's what I did.

In tech school, I met a girl. She got my interest to the point of considering marriage. After a semester of school, I announced to my parents that I was going to marry her. I packed up all of my belongings, quit school, and took my new girlfriend back home with me.

When we got there, my parents refused to let me in the house, so I turned to my drug dealer and rented an apartment from him. Besides trimming trees and doing odd jobs, I spent my time doing drugs and drinking. My girlfriend was talking about God a lot, and after a while she got tired of my drinking and drugging and went home to be with her family and go back to church. I decided I probably needed to try and clean up my act, so I moved back in with my parents and started going to church also.

The only thing was, I was still getting high and acting like a hypocrite.

After two months, my girlfriend called me to say she was moving back to town to be near me. She lived with a youth pastor and his family. The closer she got to God, the more she tried reaching out to me, but by now drugs were my god, and I just couldn't give up my addiction.

Then my girlfriend started seeing another guy. I was a wreck when she dumped me, even though I knew she had continually tried to reach out to me, and I was the fool who didn't want to give up my lifestyle for her.

The impact of losing her was overwhelming. The youth pastor suggested that I move out of state, but I couldn't. I spent four months getting wasted on cocaine instead, and my personality kept unraveling. Thoughts of suicide invaded my mind. After one very desperate night, I got in my car and drove from New York to Florida.

Changing cities did nothing to change my circumstances or my addictions. I thought that by leaving I could escape my problems, but I found other drug dealers, another set of friends to party with, and more girls to have sex with. It was the same lifestyle in a different location.

At one point I was dating a fifteen-year-old girl and a thirty-eight-year-old married woman at the same time. One night, I got a phone call from the woman's husband, a police officer, who threatened to kill me.

Again, I considered taking my own life. I was so empty inside. I decided to get my friend's gun and end my sorry life.

I dropped to the floor and started to sob.

After crying it out for a while, the Bible stories from my childhood church days started coming back to my mind. I asked God, if He was real, to change my life. There was a feeling of warmth and love and light and peace that just seemed to flood the room.

I looked at my drug scale and noticed that it was clean, and right next to it was my dust-covered Bible given to me when I was twelve years old. I had never even looked at it. I went over and picked it up. On the inside of the cover was a piece of paper that said, "God is greater than any problem I might have." I slept that night like a baby.

I had met God.

Following that eventful night, I started talking with a Christian I had met at the garage where I worked. He invited me to his church. Before too long, I got excited about going to church and reading my Bible.

My life started to improve. The craving for drugs left me. For the first time in my life, I stopped using. I moved out of my dealer's apartment and in with another Christian guy in a better neighborhood.

Three months later, I went back to New York and reconciled with my family. I asked my father and grandfather for forgiveness. In fact, it was the first time that I ever told my parents I loved them.

I also went to my cousin who had molested me and talked with him. I told him that I had forgiven him for what he had done. It was one more step in putting my past behind me.

Then I went back to Florida and stayed. I got involved with my church and started a new life. Today I am married with two children and have served as a youth pastor for almost seven years. My life is a testimony of God's grace and love and an example of the power of transformation that's possible when a messed-up, fallen-down guy meets Almighty God.[2]

It is through a transformed life that God grants us the power to save others. By the inspiration of the Holy Spirit, Paul wrote, "We have been sent to speak for Christ. It is as if God is calling to you through us. We speak for Christ when we beg you to be at peace with God" (2 Corinthians 5:20 ICB). The power of God in us is for the express purpose of bringing salvation to others.

My personal prayer has always been, "God, use me by the power of Your Spirit to save." As mind bending as it is, with this little chunk of meat called the tongue, I can use words given to me and empowered by God's Spirit that might actually change someone's eternal destiny. That's power to save like nothing we know on earth. I also have this vicarious power to save in the arena of relationships. When I use God's Word to counsel a couple in crisis, I can see a marriage saved.

Had it not been for my own transformation, I would still be the same womanizer, cocaine user, and alcoholic I was before I met Christ. But God's power transformed me into an evangelist, pastor, and teacher.

The Newness of Salvation

Salvation is redemptive, not just in terms of the kingdom of God to come, but also for our lives here and now. It's so sad to hear someone say, "I just want to enjoy my life for now. I'll give it to Jesus when I'm older and ready to leave this earth." Talk about presumption and deception! People who think that way have been shopping at the devil's store and have bought the oldest lies on the shelf.

First, none of us is guaranteed tomorrow; and second, that line of thinking shows we don't know what real life is all about. I gave up a life the world considers fun, only to discover that, in reality, it wasn't fun at all. In fact, it was killing me—relationally, financially, emotionally, physically, and spiritually.

I have never, for even one moment, regretted my decision to exchange the pleasures of this world for the treasures of God's world. I wouldn't trade my worst day as a Christian for my best day as a non-Christian. The dream I'm living out now, in God's plan for my life, far surpasses anything I planned, imagined, or hoped for in my self-driven dreams. I can't fathom why anyone would wait one second longer to begin the most joyous journey of all eternity: God's glorious dreams for us.

That journey begins with salvation. The Bible says, "If anyone is in Christ, he is a new creation; old things have passed away; behold, all things have become new" (2 Corinthians 5:17). The idea being conveyed in the original language of this verse is somewhat different than what comes across in our English translation. In English it appears that when we're saved, all things become new in a completed, past-action kind of way. It happens and that's it. But that's not it. In the original language, the idea is that our newness is ongoing. This is substantiated in another verse where the English expresses the concept more accurately: "Our physical body is becoming older and weaker, but our spirit inside us is made new every day" (2 Corinthians 4:16 ICB).

We all have good days and bad days, but we've also had great days. Being renewed daily is like having great days every day that get better and better. Some of you who are near my age may be thinking, as I sometimes have, *I'm not experiencing that many good days, let alone great days.* The problem with this thought is that it's focused on the physical.

Notice that 2 Corinthians 4:16 says that outwardly we're becoming older and weaker. That's true. It's the inward person of faith, the spiritual man or woman, who is being renewed day by day.

Have you ever noticed how drawn we are to new things? We love a new outfit or the smell of a new car. But every fashion and every automobile eventually loses its charm; they don't stay new. Salvation, on the other hand, never loses its luster. The freshness of God is inexhaustible. The Bible confirms that everything God is—all His mercy, wisdom, truth, goodness, patience, kindness, self-control, faithfulness, and perseverance—is available to us in Christ Jesus (see 1 Corinthians 1:30; Galatians 3:26; 5:22; Ephesians 1:3; 1 Timothy 1:14; 2 Timothy 2:10). It's like a limitless bank account. It's God's store, where everything we need is on the shelf. We come and say, "I need peace for today," and God says, "I've got plenty of peace." And as soon as we take our portion of peace for the day, peace appears again on the shelf. It never runs out. But we can't shop at God's store until we have been reconnected to Him through Christ—until we accept His salvation.

The Challenge of Salvation

Perhaps now you understand why sin is such a major obstacle on the path to discovering heaven's dreams for us. Sin thwarts God's purposes in our lives. Until we deal with the sin that keeps us disconnected from God, we'll never find heaven's dreams for us because they are forever entwined with God's dream. Only by humbly recognizing our helpless and hopeless condition, the futility of our self-driven dreams, and our need to reconnect with the Source of life can we receive the free gift of eternal life that restores both God's dream and ours.

As I said in the beginning of this chapter, we can't give away what we don't have. Until we have salvation, we don't have a God-given dream that empowers us to save others, because we're in the same bondage to sin as everyone else. Not until we have experienced the saving power of

71

Christ in ourselves do we have the power of Christ to affect the lives of others. How can we save someone else's marriage when our own is in trouble? How can we offer hope in the passing of a loved one if our own destiny hopelessly dies with our sin-ridden self?

God wants desperately to restore our dreams, because when He does, He then can empower us to share that salvation with others—and God will put us in positions to do so. Joseph's provision to share and power to save, which were parts of his God-given dream, would have done him no good if he had remained in prison. The humility Joseph maintained kept him connected to God, who then elevated Joseph to be in a position to save others with his provision. Contrary to our world, in which humility is counted as weakness, in God's kingdom humility is the way to exaltation: "Be humble under God's powerful hand. Then he will lift you up when the right time comes" (1 Peter 5:6 ICB).

God will exalt us at the right time for the purpose of salvation. That's the third component of a God-given dream—the position to shine—which we will explore in the next chapter.

position to *shine*

A friend of mine is a professional golfer and a Christian—he has experienced the transformation of salvation. God has placed him in a position, as a professional golfer, from which he can shine and share God's provision and power of salvation. How does he shine the light of Christ? One method he uses is writing Bible verses on all of his golf balls. When other golfers see them, they're curious. "What's this?" they ask. "Is this a Bible verse?" Then the door is open for him to shine his faith.

I've also known professional football players, baseball players, entertainers, and models who have found ways to use the positions God has placed them in to shine. They're not only living their dreams, they're also fulfilling a scriptural mandate: "Let your light so shine before men, that they may see your good works and glorify your Father in heaven" (Matthew 5:16). These people know full well who set them in their stations in life. Scripture says, "Exaltation comes neither from the east nor from the west nor from the south. But God is the Judge: He puts down one, and exalts another" (Psalm 75:6–7).

God has placed each of us in a position where someone can see us.

Our lives and our words must testify of His existence and His goodness to a watching world.

The Platform of Position

In the Bible we see that Joseph was given a position to shine forth God's greatness. Through an unlikely course of events, he went from being a favored child in a Hebrew family to being a slave of an Egyptian official, and then a prisoner. It was in that prison cell, however, that God orchestrated circumstances that eventually put Joseph in a position of power and prestige second only to Pharaoh (see Genesis 41:40).

Whatever position God gives us can be an opportunity to shine for Him as we live out our dreams. Even if we don't win the golf tournament or the ball game, even if our team ends up in last place, we'll still be in our God-given positions to shine. When we're in front of a camera and we're asked, "You lost again—how do you feel about that?" that's our God-designed opportunity to give an answer for the hope that lies within us. "Well, I may have lost this game, but let me tell you how I've won at this game called *life*." We still can glorify God because our position to shine is not dependent on the temporal conditions of winning or losing.

Our corporate dream as believers should be for the bank account of every church and every believer to contain provision sufficient to share with those in need. The pulpits of our churches and the words of our mouths should proclaim God's power to save. Then the positive-impact churches and individual Christians have on their communities will help establish their positions to shine their lights for Christ.

Our church purchased a piece of property in Fort Lauderdale, Florida, in 1995. Over the years, as attendance increased, we had to have a new traffic light installed to make it easier for people to come and go from the church property. With the responsibility and cost of adding the light came the privilege of naming the cross street that exits Cypress

Creek Road and turns onto the property. What did we call it? Calvary Chapel—that's what the sign says. And everyone who drives on Cypress Creek Road through that intersection has the opportunity to observe how God has blessed Calvary Chapel Fort Lauderdale.

It's not every day that a church is set on seventy-five acres and has its own street sign. I hope you hear my heart and realize that I'm not bragging about our church. I'm making a point. When people stop at that light and think, *So that's where Calvary Chapel is. A friend of mine went to that church. Wow, they have their own traffic light. That's pretty amazing*, that's our position to shine. It's our opportunity to let the world know that God is into grand displays of His glory. His main purpose for Calvary Chapel is for us to be a place where people can find provision and salvation and where they can observe us living out our God-given dreams as a church. And all who come through our doors can find their God-given dreams as well. That's why we put *Calvary Chapel* on that street sign. We wanted to display the glory of God.

A Good Look at God's Glory

God loves to show off His glory. We see this clearly in the story of Moses and the children of Israel, which we looked at earlier. Centuries after the death of Joseph, when another Pharaoh had enslaved the Hebrews, and after ten major miracles, Pharaoh finally let God's people go. But they were barely gone when Pharaoh had a change of heart. By the time the Israelites had arrived at the Red Sea, Pharaoh and his army were closing in fast.

From Israel's limited perspective, the situation looked bad. Not so from God's perspective. He knew exactly what He was doing. In fact, it was His plan to bring the Israelites to this very spot so that He could gain glory. We see this in the instructions God gave to Moses: "'Tell the Israelites to turn back and encamp near Pi Hahiroth, between Migdol and the sea. They are to encamp by the sea, directly opposite Baal

Zephon. Pharaoh will think, "The Israelites are wandering around the land in confusion, hemmed in by the desert." And I will harden Pharaoh's heart, and he will pursue them. But I will gain glory for myself through Pharaoh and all his army, and the Egyptians will know that I am the LORD'" (Exodus 14:2–4 NIV).

So what does God's glory look like? Check it out just a few verses later:

The angel of God, who had been traveling in front of Israel's army, withdrew and went behind them. The pillar of cloud also moved from in front and stood behind them, coming between the armies of Egypt and Israel. Throughout the night the cloud brought darkness to the one side and light to the other side; so neither went near the other all night long.

Then Moses stretched out his hand over the sea, and all that night the LORD drove the sea back with a strong east wind and turned it into dry land. The waters were divided, and the Israelites went through the sea on dry ground, with a wall of water on their right and on their left.

The Egyptians pursued them, and all Pharaoh's horses and chariots and horsemen followed them into the sea. During the last watch of the night the LORD looked down from the pillar of fire and cloud at the Egyptian army and threw it into confusion. He made the wheels of their chariots come off so that they had difficulty driving. And the Egyptians said, "Let's get away from the Israelites! The LORD is fighting for them against Egypt."

Then the LORD said to Moses, "Stretch out your hand over the sea so that the waters may flow back over the Egyptians and their chariots and horsemen." Moses stretched out his hand over the sea, and at daybreak the sea went back to its place. The Egyptians were fleeing toward it, and the LORD swept them into the sea. The water flowed back and covered the chariots and horsemen—the entire army of Pharaoh that had followed the Israelites into the sea. Not one of them survived.

But the Israelites went through the sea on dry ground, with a wall
of water on their right and on their left. That day the LORD saved Israel
from the hands of the Egyptians, and Israel saw the Egyptians lying dead
on the shore. And when the Israelites saw the great power the LORD dis-
played against the Egyptians, the people feared the LORD and put their
trust in him and in Moses his servant. (Exodus 14:19–31 NIV)

God pulls off the miraculous so we can stand in awe of Him and
trust that He is able to take care of us. We read a great deal about God's
glory in Scripture, and it is His glory that we are to display when given
the position to shine. In the New Testament Paul wrote, "This truth is
Christ himself, who is in you. He is our only hope for glory" (Colossians
1:27 ICB). The fact that Christ is in us is the reason we can shine forth
the glory of God.

Let's take a closer look at exactly what God's glory is. Moses was so
fascinated with it that in Exodus 33:18 he asked God, "Please, show me
Your glory." God put him in the cleft of a rock and passed by him, and
Moses saw His loving-kindness, grace, goodness, and compassion (see
Exodus 34:6–7)—the essence of who God is.

Parallel Moses's experience with John 14:13, when Jesus said,
"Whatever you ask in My name, that I will do, that the Father may be
glorified in the Son." This gives a unique perspective on the purpose of
prayer. When we pray for our God-given dreams to be fulfilled, we're
giving God access to our lives so He can perfect a work in us that will
bring glory to Him. The loving-kindness, grace, goodness, and compassion that mark God's glory will flow through our lives.

Does it surprise you that Jesus says we can ask for whatever we
want? Isn't He concerned at all about what we'll ask for?

No, not really.

In His sovereignty, God can use even our desires to declare His
glory. Prosperity, popularity, and power can all be platforms to give

glory to God. You could be a professional athlete like my friend who paints Bible verses on his golf balls. You could be CEO of a major corporation, like Chick-fil-A's S. Truett Cathy, who used his platform as a successful businessman to make a statement that his relationship with God was more important than doing business on Sunday. Or you can be a wonderful mom who sticks to her guns, insisting that her kids be respectful, and who limits their intake of worldly and ungodly things so their excellent behavior is noticed by all.

Whatever our positions—wherever we have authority, power, prosperity, or popularity—we are people others look up to, listen to, and imitate because we've been successful at what we do. And we can use that success to give glory to God.

Competitive Christians

God is not against getting to the top. As much as I loathe how sin has distorted and perverted competition, in reality it's God who has given us a competitive spirit. Knowing this helps us understand that the problem is not competition. We can actually be competitive for God.

What does it mean to have a competitive spirit for God? An example would be the response of one church to another church down the block that put on a Christmas cantata one year. Seeing that church's success, the first church began planning its own Christmas event. Pretty soon other churches were vying for the spotlight, and all the while God was being glorified to a greater and greater degree. It was Hebrews 10:24 in action: "Let us consider one another in order to stir up love and good works." As each church is challenged by the efforts of another, the gospel message goes out to more and more people in the community.

We see examples of competition in Scripture too. Why did John feel the need to note that he outran Peter to the tomb? (see John 20:4). Why was it important that we know there were 153 fish in the net—one of the biggest catches the disciples had ever had? (see John 21:11). Why did God note for us that when Peter preached, three thousand people were added to the church in one day? (see Acts 2:41). Throughout Scripture attention is given to numbers and facts that help us to see that pomp, size, and the grandiose are all platforms from which God can be given glory. There's nothing wrong with competition in this sense.

A proper competitive spirit can also be good for the body of Christ. Healthy competition can spur believers to love and good deeds (see Hebrews 10:24), to exhort one another daily (see Hebrews 3:13), and to be an example to other believers in speech, in life, in love, in faith, and in purity (see 1 Timothy 4:12).

As we discovered in chapter 2, Proverbs 27:17 ("As iron sharpens iron, so one man sharpens another" NIV) indicates that something wonderful should happen when two Christians who love the Lord get together in conversation. It should be a time of refreshing, strengthening, encouraging, and maybe even some healthy competing.

> Throughout Scripture attention is given to numbers and facts that help us to see that pomp, size, and the grandiose are all platforms from which God can be given glory.

I recently called one of the pastors from another large church in our community, Larry Thompson, at First Baptist Church, wanting to know how his congregation was responding to their *Purpose-Driven Life* project. I was curious to know what effect it was having on the body of Christ at his church. Why? Well, it's interesting to know about other people and programs, but mostly it's because I've come to realize that as I care for the flock of God, I must become, by default, a church-growth expert. I want and need to know when something is good for the local body of believers and able to make it grow.

Interest in what will make something grow or succeed is not unique to the pastorate. Anyone who takes his or her mission in life seriously is interested in ways to better fulfill that mission. If we sit for just a few moments with horse enthusiasts at a horse show, we'll learn everything from the best health supplements for horses to the best farrier to see about shoeing a horse. These people love their horses, they want the best for them, and they'll go to great lengths to get it.

I love the people God has brought to our church, I want the best for His flock, and I'll go to great lengths to get it. That's what makes me want to know what other pastors are doing for their church bodies to help them become healthier and holier. It's something I will always take an interest in and be competitive for in a good way.

Apart from God, however, a competitive spirit gives birth to anxiety, contention, frustration, and all the negative things we've come to associate with competition. We were all shocked some time ago when we learned of Tanya Harding's desperate measures against Nancy Kerrigan to increase her own chances of winning the Olympic gold medal in figure skating.

Unfortunately, that wrong spirit of competition can even get into the body of Christ. Recently a magazine called *Outreach* listed our church as one of the fastest-growing churches in America. It was an honor to be on the cover of this magazine and to look at where our church was positioned on the list of the top one hundred churches in the United States. But I knew that every pastor who looked at that list might start thinking, "What would it take for my church to be number one?"

While that ambition can be holy, it can also be vain. It's one thing to want church growth when it comes from a desire to see more souls won for the kingdom of God. It's quite a different spirit, however, when our ambition stems from wanting more recognition and power.

In his first letter to the church at Corinth, the apostle Paul dealt with this human ambition to be better than everyone else: "My brothers, some from Chloe's household have informed me that there are quarrels among you. What I mean is this: One of you says, 'I follow Paul'; another, 'I follow Apollos'; another, 'I follow Cephas'; still another, 'I follow Christ.' Is Christ divided? Was Paul crucified for you? Were you baptized into the name of Paul?" (1 Corinthians 1:11–13 NIV). Paul rebuked the Corinthian church for their unhealthy spirit of competition. Self-centered competition can be detected by the division it causes in the body of Christ.

The Drive of Divine Design

Only in our fallen nature does the competitive spirit follow a destructive path. In our redeemed nature, it is the Lord who drives us to want to be better or do more. When we're seeking heaven's dreams and God's plans for our lives, He redeems this spirit of competition for His use. And how does He use it?

To answer that question, let's consider what Paul wrote to the Corinthians: "Think of what you were when you were called. Not many of you were wise by human standards; not many were influential; not many were of noble birth. But God chose the foolish things of the world to shame the wise; God chose the weak things of the world to shame the strong" (1 Corinthians 1:26–27 NIV).

Paul wasn't emphasizing what the Corinthian believers lacked. His focus was on the truth that God wants to save everyone, regardless of how worthy or unworthy they might seem or feel. God wants to save popular and unpopular people, powerful and weak people, and prosperous and destitute people. He often does that by making His glory shine through things this world counts foolish, thereby confounding the wise.

I'm a living example of this. I was shocked that I even graduated from high school. I have no formal education or training to do what I do. Yet in God's wisdom, and to His glory alone, I now pastor one of the fastest growing churches in America. That irony still makes me chuckle every time I think about it.

I have a blast with church-growth experts who come to interview me. They always ask what we've done to make the church grow. When I tell them that we've never advertised, I have no formal training, we don't collect an offering, we teach strictly from the Bible, and we don't even have an official membership; they scratch their heads. They tell me that based on known facts concerning church growth, this (the success of Calvary Chapel Fort Lauderdale) shouldn't have happened.

I agree, and that's why God gets all the glory. When God uses foolish, ignoble nobodies, the world can see beyond a shadow of doubt that the glory belongs to God. I'm elated that this church is not built on Bob Coy. If it were a work of my own doing, for my own glory, it would die with me because my glory won't last. But as a product of God's glory, this church can survive my limited time here on earth.

The Vanishing Glory of Man

Time after time I've witnessed the emptiness and misery of men and women who had money, power, and prestige. One celebrity confided that he could never be sure if someone was a real friend, or if a woman was really interested in him for who he was, or if people were only in his life because of his wealth and fame. He realized that no matter how much money he had, he couldn't buy love. Though he was popular, he lacked true friends. His "glory" didn't measure up, even remotely, to God's glory. Human glory is elusive and unsatisfying, even when we're in the middle of it.

If God entrusts me with a large and influential church, He is simply giving me a platform—a position from which I can bring Him glory by shining His light into the world around me. It's not because I'm someone special; it's because the Lord is special.

The Platform of Suffering

The bottom line is that God is looking for avenues through which He can gain glory, but these avenues don't always have to come through our successes. God often gains even greater glory from the platform of our adversity.

The apostle Paul wrote, "He [the Lord] said to me, 'My grace is sufficient for you, for My strength is made perfect in weakness.' Therefore most gladly I will rather boast in my infirmities, that the power of Christ may rest upon me" (2 Corinthians 12:9). If any man lived who knew intimately this alternate avenue of shining, it was Paul. From shipwrecks to beatings to stonings, he lived a life of sacrifice and hardship through which God's glory was clearly displayed.

This same platform of suffering sets apart the book of Job as one of the more glorious books of the Bible. How many of us have read the trials of Job and then felt inspired by his words: "'Naked I came from my mother's womb, and naked shall I return there. The LORD gave, and the LORD has taken away; blessed be the name of the LORD'" (Job 1:21). Job understood that through his suffering, God was giving him a platform to shine—and shine he did. Few people, even in Scripture, have demonstrated the level of unwavering faith Job did.

I find it noteworthy that in the very first chapter of Job, we learn that he was righteous. We know from the start that his trials were not a result of his own dumb decisions, as many of ours can be. Yet through all his pain and suffering, Job never charged God with wrongdoing (see Job 1:22). This doesn't mean he didn't have questions or that he was thrilled with what was going on in his life; it simply means that he patiently endured his trial, trusting that God would somehow vindicate him. And in the end, God did. In an amazing discourse that covers four chapters, God used the platform of Job's suffering to show all of us His glory.

Then, when God had finished speaking to Job, He turned to Job's friend Eliphaz and said: "I am angry with you and your two friends, because you have not spoken of me what is right, as my servant Job has" (Job 42:7 NIV).

During his suffering, Job probably had no idea his unfailing faith would be used to show God's glory to his family and friends and to countless others throughout the ages. How many of us would be willing participants in bringing God glory in such a painful, difficult way, even knowing that in the heat of a trial, our faith is most visible? Sometimes God doesn't put us in positions of power, prestige, or affluence. Sometimes He places us in positions of difficulty and testing because His grace is sufficient, and His strength is shown most perfectly in our weakness (see 2 Corinthians 12:9).

> When we show grace by expressing joy and faith in His goodness during our trials, we manifest the glory and essence of God.

God's grace is part of who He is. So when we show grace by expressing joy and faith in His goodness during our trials, we manifest the glory and essence of God. God's grace abounded so much in the life of Paul that he could say: "I have been crucified with Christ; it is no longer I who live, but Christ lives in me; and the life which I now live in the flesh I live by faith in the Son of God, who loved me and gave Himself for me. I do not set aside the grace of God; for if righteousness comes through the law, then Christ died in vain" (Galatians 2:20–21).

When we go through trials—the loss of a loved one, financial hardship, a disabling health problem, divorce, betrayal—and still exhibit the joy of our salvation, we bring God glory. Our strength in times of trial and temptation is what convinces people that our faith and our God are real. Many people can shine in the midst of success or prosperity, but would they shine as brightly in the midst of suffering? How a believer handles adversity should stand in stark contrast to how an unbeliever handles it.

I witnessed this difference dramatically during a recent hospital visit. I called on someone from our fellowship who had lost a leg. When I walked into the room, I encountered a strong, faith-filled man. He kept talking about trusting God and how he was looking forward to seeing how God would use him in the midst of his trial. We had a delightful time of fellowship. But before I left the hospital, I went to the next room to visit a man who had suffered a similar injury. I was dumbstruck by the contrast. When I started to enter this man's room, he actually threw something at me and shouted, "Get out of here! I don't want anything to do with a God who would do this to me."

The character of Lieutenant Dan in *Forrest Gump* came vividly to mind after that experience. In the movie, Forrest saved the life of Lieutenant Dan in Vietnam. Unfortunately, Lieutenant Dan lost both his legs and ended up a bitter and frustrated person who just wanted to die. Then one day he and Forrest were out on the ocean in their shrimp boat and a severe storm blew up. In the midst of that storm, Lieutenant Dan climbed to the top of the mast and railed against God, challenging Him to a showdown.

In the next scene we see a different Lieutenant Dan. He still has no legs, but now he has no anger, bitterness, or resentment either. He appears to finally be at peace. What made the difference? Forrest tells us in one of those lines he's become so famous for: "He never said so, but I think Lieutenant Dan made his peace with God." Lieutenant Dan had found the glory of God through the hardship in his life and then was able to manifest the *doxa*—the very essence—of God.

The Platform of Impossibility

So many times in our lives, God has to strip us of all those things that promote self-sufficiency so that others—and even we ourselves—can see His handiwork and sufficiency in the circumstances of our lives. He may do this through suffering, as in the case of Job and Lieutenant Dan. Other times He accomplishes the same goal through impossible circumstances, as with Gideon.

The story of Gideon in the book of Judges is a classic example of how God takes us to a place of impossibility so it will be obvious to all that He is the One who deserves credit for our success. Gideon was given the task of delivering the Israelites from the Midianites and the Amalekites, fearsome desert nomads who repeatedly raided Israel, destroying its crops, plundering its wealth, and then escaping back into the desert with such speed that the Israelites couldn't stop them. In fact, when we first encounter Gideon, we find him hiding from the Midianites, fearfully threshing wheat in a wine press.

As we can well imagine, when God called Gideon, He did not find an eager volunteer. Although Gideon knew the will of God, he tested God twice by laying out a fleece and imposing impossible standards of proof in what seems to have been an effort to avoid doing what God had called him to do. God met Gideon's conditions both times and then gave him the strategy that would guarantee victory for Israel.

Gideon called all the able-bodied men he could gather to fight against the enemy. The thirty-two thousand men who followed Gideon seemed no match for the 135,000 men Midian and Amalek mustered. I can't fathom what must have gone through Gideon's mind when he considered the odds, but I'm sure it wasn't even close to the panic he felt when the Lord spoke to him again and said, "The people who are with you are too many for Me to give the Midianites into their hands, lest

Israel claim glory for itself against Me, saying, 'My own hand has saved me'" (Judges 7:2).

To reduce their number, God prescribed two elimination criteria to weed out some of the men in Gideon's army. First, Gideon was to allow those who were afraid to fight to leave. Second, he was to take the remaining army to a water hole. Those who knelt down to get a drink of water were sent home. I would love to have seen the look on Gideon's face when he surveyed the remaining three hundred men. One almost has to wonder if God wasn't getting Gideon back a little for the whole fleece episode.

Once God had reduced Gideon's army to just three hundred men, He gave Gideon what has to be one of the most bizarre war strategies ever. The men were given pitchers, torches, and trumpets and stationed around the Midianite encampment. At Gideon's signal they were to break the pitchers so the torchlight would become visible, and sound the trumpets to give the enemy the impression that they were surrounded by a much larger army.

What was the result of this audacious game plan? The Midianite army ran, their leaders were killed, the Midianite oppression ended, and you'd better believe that no one who knew the game plan could take credit for the victory. Every Israelite knew that the glory for that battle belonged to God. In the face of the impossible, there is only one explanation for success: it has to be God.

Have you ever considered that when you face impossible circumstances in your life, when your dreams of success seem so distant and unattainable, that maybe—just maybe—God is setting you up for an awesome display of His glory?

I ask this because the events of my own journey toward my dream bear this out. When the church consisted of only fifty people, I never would have believed that God would do what He has. It never crossed my mind that He could use my absolute inability to display His absolute capability, but that's exactly what happened.

Now, some twenty years later, my position to shine is helping others to shine. The spotlight is on us at Calvary Chapel Fort Lauderdale, and we're taking every opportunity to proclaim the power of God's salvation and the abundance of His provision. We're working toward that day when we will hear Him say, "Well done, my good and faithful servants."

I envision it being somewhat like when my daughter comes to present me with a huge drawing she has just finished and says, "Dad, this is for you." As I take it in my hand, holding it up to admire it, I look at her, and she looks at me. Her smile spreads from ear to ear because she did something with which she knows I am well pleased. Her face shines because she senses my pleasure in what she has done.

I want to feel that in my relationship with God—that I did something for Him with which He is well pleased, and because of that I'm shining.

Joseph's Platform

Joseph is one of the rare characters in Scripture who had the privilege of shining both in triumph and in tragedy. The thread of enduring trials with faithfulness and joy runs throughout his story. Though he had been betrayed by his brothers, sold into slavery, double-crossed by his boss's wife, and forgotten by the cupbearer and baker, it seems Joseph never lost sight of God's goodness. And then, when the time was right, God exalted him to a position of power and prestige where he continued to bring God glory.

What we may not see as readily is the silent, steady undercurrent of evil that dogged Joseph. In the destructive jealousy of his brothers and the lust of Potiphar's wife, Joseph's dream was being attacked by an unseen enemy. This same foe dogs our pursuit of heaven's dreams, waiting at every turn to discourage, defeat, and destroy what God is doing in our lives. Whether we succeed in staying the course of our journeys to the end depends greatly on our recognizing this unseen adversary. The Bible reveals his identity with a strong warning not to underestimate him: "Be sober, be vigilant; because your adversary the devil walks about like a roaring lion, seeking whom he may devour" (1 Peter 5:8).

In chapter 1, I challenged some ideas about God. In the next chapter, I want to pose the same challenge to our ideas about the devil, because I believe he has been highly successful in keeping his real identity hidden behind a red suit, a goatee, and a pitchfork. If that's what you think of when I say, "Satan," then you're sitting in the lion's den and don't even know it. You'd better read on.

Part Two

Hell's *Nightmare*

the hate behind the *nightmare*

Just as we need to clear the slate of all preconceived ideas concerning God, so it behooves us to do so when it comes to Satan. From childhood stories of the bogeyman to Hollywood horror flicks, the devil has been presented in caricature that doesn't necessarily match up with reality. In this chapter we'll learn the facts about our opponent from One who knows him better than anyone else does and has been enduring hell's nightmare—Satan's hatred and attacks—since before God spoke the first ray of light into existence.

A Biblical View of Satan

I'm not really sure where the image of Satan with a red suit, goatee, and pitchfork came from, but it certainly wasn't from the Bible. Far from being grotesque and evil in appearance, Scripture tells us that Lucifer was among God's most perfect and beautiful creations. In Ezekiel 28 we find a description. The chapter starts out talking about the King of Tyre, but midway through, the text takes on a dual meaning. Some Bible scholars suggest that since the King of Tyre was never in the Garden of Eden, nor was he ever a guardian cherub, the text actually shifts to describing Satan.

Part Two: Hell's *Nightmare*

In this area of Scripture we find references to Lucifer's body's being adorned with precious gems and his mountings being made of gold:

Son of man, take up a lament concerning the king of Tyre and say to him:

"This is what the Sovereign LORD *says:*

'You were the model of perfection,
full of wisdom and perfect in beauty.

You were in Eden,
the garden of God;
every precious stone adorned you:
ruby, topaz and emerald,
chrysolite, onyx and jasper,
sapphire, turquoise and beryl.

Your settings and mountings were made of gold;
on the day you were created they were prepared.

You were anointed as a guardian cherub,
for so I ordained you.

You were on the holy mount of God;
you walked among the fiery stones.

You were blameless in your ways
from the day you were created
till wickedness was found in you.

Through your widespread trade
you were filled with violence,
and you sinned.

So I drove you in disgrace from the mount of God,
and I expelled you, O guardian cherub,

from among the fiery stones.

Your heart became proud
  on account of your beauty,
  and you corrupted your wisdom
  because of your splendor.

So I threw you to the earth;

I made a spectacle of you before kings.'" (Ezekiel 28:12–17 NIV)

Satan was anything but ugly. His body was fashioned of precious gems and gold. He was the model of perfection and perfect in beauty. Perhaps it was his beauty that contributed to his downfall by filling him with pride. And perhaps it is this discrepancy between what most of the world believes Satan looks like and what he truly looks like that allows him to masquerade as an angel of light (see 2 Corinthians 11:14), deceiving so many into believing that he doesn't really exist. Since they don't see the guy in the red suit with the goatee and pitchfork, they figure he's just a figment of some theologian's imagination who was probably out of touch with reality anyway. The amazing thing to consider, however, is that even with so many people denying the personal existence of Satan, more than seven million Web links come up when his name is typed into the Google search engine on the Internet. That's a lot of activity for someone who doesn't exist.

The truth is that he does exist, and he's got an agenda that is diametrically opposed to God's dreams for us. If we're ever going to succeed in discovering the reality of heaven's dreams in our lives, we need to face the fact that Satan and other demons do exist and are formidable foes. We need to understand who Satan is—and who he is not.

Contrary to popular belief, Satan is not God's evil counterpart. The Bible firmly establishes that only God is self-existent and infinite (see Isaiah 43:10). Satan, on the other hand, is a created being and has many limitations (see Ezekiel 28:15; Job 2:6; Romans 16:20). God is omniscient, omnipotent, and sovereign. That means any knowledge, power, or dominion Satan has is given to him by the express permission of God and kept within the limits God has fixed, as we see in Job 1:12 and 2:6.

Although we should never mistake Satan for God's equal, we should be careful not to underestimate him. His name, *Satan*, meaning "adversary," is significant. He is our adversary, and like any opponent we expect to defeat, it's vital that we know his capabilities and strategy. In subsequent chapters we'll look more closely at his strategy, but in this chapter we will examine who it is we are fighting against and, though it may surprise you, who it is that's fighting against us, and why.

> We are the objects of God's affection, and thus Satan has made it his goal to destroy us.

Satan is a fallen angel who has pitted himself against God and anyone who belongs to God. While he's not omnipotent, angels are far more powerful than human beings (see 2 Peter 2:11). In Revelation 7:1 we learn that it will take only four angels to hold back all the wind from the earth. For those of us who survived Hurricane Andrew, this is quite a testimony to their power. In a more terrifying display of these powerful beings, Revelation 9:15 describes four angels who are able to destroy one-third of mankind.

We also see from Job 1:12–19 that God gave Satan power to control the forces of nature—at least temporarily—and incite the hearts of men. He can hinder our plans, as he did the apostle Paul's in 1 Thessalonians 2:18.

During Christ's temptation in the wilderness, Satan claimed to have authority over all the kingdoms of the earth, along with the power to assign that authority to whomever he wishes (Luke 4:5–6). (Jesus neither denied nor acknowledged this claim.)

We discover in the parable of the weeds (Matthew 13:37–43) that the devil is able to plant demonic decoys within the body of Christ. Satan and these decoys will look like the real deal: "Satan himself masquerades as an angel of light. It is not surprising, then, if his servants masquerade as servants of righteousness. Their end will be what their actions deserve" (2 Corinthians 11:14–15 NIV).

Satan's Hostility toward God

Satan's agenda is to rob, kill, steal, and destroy (see John 10:10), to devour (see 1 Peter 5:8), and to deceive (see 2 Corinthians 11:3) mankind. Why are we his target? The answer to that question gives even clearer insight into his wickedness and why we cannot opt out of the battle.

Satan cannot harm God directly because he's under God's sovereign control. So he strikes at the heart of what is most precious to God—us. We are the objects of God's affection, and thus Satan has made it his goal to destroy us.

It isn't hard for me to imagine how effective this method is when I think of someone trying to get to me through my kids. I could probably withstand ridicule, rejection, or any other behavior harmful to me to a much greater degree than I could handle the same behavior toward my children. It's tolerable to turn the other cheek when the slap is to my own face, but I must be painfully honest and say that if someone struck one of my kids, I'd probably level him.

God is no different. He takes offenses toward His children quite personally: "This is what the Lord of heaven's armies says: 'Whoever hurts you hurts what is precious to me'" (Zechariah 2:8 ICB).

Although God is all powerful, He doesn't guarantee our salvation; instead, He gives us a choice to accept or reject His redemption. His sovereignty could raise Christ from the dead, but it will not interfere with our right to say no to His gracious offer of eternal life. And it's in the arena of free will where Satan has such success against us. Through all the tricks in his unrighteous little bag, and because of his passionate hatred of God, he continues to dupe and deceive some people into choosing death over life.

At this point I wouldn't blame you for deciding you don't want to get involved in what seems to be a personal matter between God and Satan. Unfortunately, we don't have a choice.

The battle is raging, and we are the bounty over which the war is being fought. Every human being must, with his or her free will, choose a side. Jesus affirmed this when He drew the battle line and made it very clear: "If anyone is not with me, then he is against me. He who does not work with me is working against me" (Matthew 12:30 ICB).

Some may be reading this and thinking, *I don't know if I even believe in this spiritual battle thing.* Be careful! Just as the Enemy tries to make us think he's not real, so he also tries to make us think there is no battle, and that only what we see is real. Nothing could be further from the truth.

The battle is real, and the Bible tells us that even though it's a war that can't be seen, we're fighting it all the time. We may think we're up against a tough boss or an indifferent spouse, but God says we're actually up against hell itself: "We are not fighting against people made of flesh and blood, but against the evil rulers and authorities of the unseen world, against those mighty powers of darkness who rule this world, and against wicked spirits in the heavenly realms" (Ephesians 6:12 NLT).

Make no mistake: the spiritual realm is as real, if not more so, than the realm in which we can see, hear, smell, taste, and feel. The spiritual realm will endure for eternity, while our own world will eventually pass away: "So we set our eyes not on what we see but on what we cannot see. What we see will last only a short time. But what we cannot see will last forever" (2 Corinthians 4:18 ICB).

Like it or not, Satan is real. We are in the battle, and if we dare to lay hold of heaven's dreams for our lives, we will surely be subject to attack.

Now you understand why Satan is the ultimate dream buster. He can't defeat God, so he settles for attacking and attempting to destroy the objects of God's affection—us. His sole purpose in this world is to throw us off course, to keep us from finding and fulfilling the dreams God has for us, which is why I mentioned in the introduction to this book that we have to fight for God's dream.

The good news is that our battle has already been won, and the victory is ours for the taking: "You belong to God, my dear children. You have already won your fight with these false prophets, because the Spirit who lives in you is greater than the spirit who lives in the world" (1 John 4:4 NLT). God has stacked the deck in our favor and limited the devil's activity.

After several years in ministry, I've discovered that the Enemy has a very small bag of tricks. He has finite resources and strategies for his deception. Oddly enough, he's successful even with these limited methods because they work so well on most people. Satan takes our dreams and, before we've even had a chance to establish or express them, he crushes them.

Satan's MO

One of my more vivid memories as a child was of the flying monkeys in *The Wizard of Oz*. I hated them, not just because they were scary, but because of what they did. While Dorothy, the Scarecrow, the Cowardly Lion, and the Tin Man were trying to realize their dreams in the Land of Oz, these monkeys swooped in, wreaked havoc, and took them off course.

The people of Israel experienced a similar phenomenon, as we see in Numbers 13. Their flying monkeys came in the form of giants in the

Promised Land. Moses sent twelve spies into the land of Canaan with the following instructions: "Go up this way into the South, and go up to the mountains, and see what the land is like: whether the people who dwell in it are strong or weak, few or many; whether the land they dwell in is good or bad; whether the cities they inhabit are like camps or strongholds; whether the land is rich or poor; and whether there are forests there or not. Be of good courage. And bring some of the fruit of the land" (Numbers 13:17–20).

The twelve spies came back with this report:

"We went to the land where you sent us. It truly flows with milk and honey, and this is its fruit. Nevertheless the people who dwell in the land are strong; the cities are fortified and very large; moreover we saw the descendants of Anak there. . . ."

Then Caleb quieted the people before Moses, and said, "Let us go up at once and take possession, for we are well able to overcome it."

But the men who had gone up with him said, "We are not able to go up against the people, for they are stronger than we." And they gave the children of Israel a bad report of the land which they had spied out, saying, "The land through which we have gone as spies is a land that devours its inhabitants, and all the people whom we saw in it are men of great stature. There we saw the giants (the descendants of Anak came from the giants); and we were like grasshoppers in our own sight, and so we were in their sight." (Numbers 13:27–33)

Like the flying monkeys in Oz that stood between Dorothy and her dream of going home, the giants in Canaan posed a seemingly insurmountable obstacle to Israel's dream of entering and living in the Promised Land. We've all encountered "flying monkeys" that appear out of nowhere and swoop down to work their evil against us. Whether it's a dart of doubt, a word of discouragement, a detour, or a dead-end,

Satan uses his deceitful tactics to drag us off course and keep us from achieving our dreams.

Flying monkeys are successful largely because they stir up fear in their victims. Fear is a strong motivator of human behavior. More than that, when we consider that worship is ardent devotion, honoring and esteeming something or someone, we see that fear is, at least by definition, a form of worship. When we fear something, we're actually esteeming it, giving it the honor of our attention, and devoting our concern to it.

God expects us to fear Him in this sense of esteem and devotion: "What does the LORD your God require of you? He requires you to fear him, to live according to his will, to love and worship him with all your heart and soul" (Deuteronomy 10:12 NLT). He places such importance on this that He even keeps a book of the names of those who fear Him: "Those who feared the LORD spoke to one another, and the LORD listened and heard them; so a book of remembrance was written before Him for those who fear the LORD and who meditate on His name" (Malachi 3:16).

When we understand the motivational impact of fear, it's easy to comprehend why it's important to fear God. Typically what we fear dictates how we behave. For example, our universal fear of death has motivated us to create safeguards in society that work on our behalf, such as laws that prohibit one person from killing another, or restrictions on pharmaceuticals that could be harmful, or even limitations on extreme sports that reduce the risk of death.

Fear can also be a negative stimulus. Many people limit their ability to enjoy life because they're afraid to fly. This fear can be so overwhelming that a loving mother will refuse to attend her son or daughter's wedding if air travel is the only way to get there. Her fear of flying overrides her love and deepest maternal instincts.

Considering the power of fear to change our behavior positively or negatively, it's no wonder God says we're wise if we fear Him: "The fear of the Lord, that is wisdom, and to depart from evil is understanding" (Job 28:28).

But Satan capitalizes on fear and the power it wields over us. He witnessed fear's immense influence immediately after the first sin in the Garden of Eden. When he originally approached Adam and Eve, they showed no sign of fear because they'd had nothing to be afraid of up to that time. They were ensconced in God's protective, perfect love. Once Adam and Eve bought the devil's lie and ate the forbidden fruit, however, they became keenly aware of themselves and their own guilt. They felt a growing sense of dread that they'd never experienced before—fear.

How do we know this? Let's look at Adam's conversation with God after the Fall, when the Lord called for him in the Garden: "The LORD God called to Adam and said to him, 'Where are you?' So he said, 'I heard Your voice in the garden, and *I was afraid* because I was naked; and I hid myself'" (Genesis 3:9–10, emphasis added).

From the moment they disobeyed, Adam and Eve were marked by the consequence of sin: "When Adam sinned, sin entered the entire human race. Adam's sin brought death, so death spread to everyone" (Romans 5:12 NLT). Death entered through their sin, and the first thing to die was their innocence. No longer could Adam and Eve—nor can we, for that matter—enjoy life without knowing evil and the fear it brings. From that moment to this present day, Satan has manipulated the human race by exploiting the fear that accompanies our knowledge of evil.

He did it in my life for years. I wasn't always a public speaker. In fact, I once suffered from agoraphobia. It wasn't unusual for me to suffer panic attacks when I was asked to speak in front of people. My phobia was so bad that at one point I didn't leave my apartment for a month.

chapter 5: the hate behind the *nightmare*

The first time I faced my fear of public speaking, as a Christian, was when my pastor at Calvary Chapel Las Vegas asked me to make the announcements. Just the thought of doing that made me physically ill, but because I wanted desperately to do whatever God asked of me, I agreed. Unfortunately, that first experience was not a victorious one. Right before I was supposed to take the microphone, I realized that I had no moisture in my mouth—probably because it had all gone to my hands in a profuse sweat. I'd love to say that I pressed through that fear, but I didn't. I ran out of the sanctuary, and my pastor made the announcements.

Despite this first failure, it wasn't long before he asked me again to speak before the congregation. This time he wanted me to give the altar call after our movie night. I knew God wanted me to take the challenge, so I got on my face in my living room to get before His face in the throne room. I knew that to be able to do what God was asking of me, I was going to need His strength. As I prayed, worshiping intently as a Keith Green song played on my stereo, the lyrics jumped out at me like the voice of God:

God's calling, and you're the one

But like Jonah you run

He's told you to speak

But you keep holding it in,

Oh can't you see it's such a sin?

The world is sleeping in the dark

That the church just can't fight

Cause it's asleep in the light

Part Two: Hell's *Nightmare*

How can you be so dead

When you've been so well fed?

Jesus rose from the grave

And you, you can't even get out of bed

Oh, Jesus rose from the dead

Come on, get out of your bed[1]

It was then that I had my "Garden of Gethsemane" experience. It became a "not my will but Yours be done" defining moment. I left that prayer time with the commitment that if I died presenting the gospel at the movie night, at least I would enter heaven seeing God's smiling face.

I sat through the entire movie with a knot bigger than Texas in my stomach. Then I reluctantly but obediently stepped up and took the microphone, which I held tightly against my lips so people wouldn't see them twitching. If that wasn't bad enough, only a few minutes into it, I realized I would have to sit down because my knees were knocking so hard from fright, I thought I was going to fall over. Through all of this, I continued to share the words God was giving me, although I was pretty sure no one would even listen, let alone respond at the end.

As I gave the invitation, I turned my back to the audience so as to avoid the humiliation of no one coming forward. I told them I was going to kneel at the altar, and they could come forward to pray with me if they wanted to accept Christ. You can't even begin to imagine my shock when I realized that people were actually coming forward and kneeling next to me. In spite of my twitching lips, knocking knees, and lack of faith, God orchestrated kingdom business through a fearful but willing vessel.

I learned a lesson that night that will carry me through the rest of my life. No matter how ominous something looks, and no matter how afraid or incapable I feel, with God all things are possible. It was even possible that a man like me, who had been taken captive by a monstrous fear, could be liberated to speak truth and bring freedom to thousands of others.

That's my story, but I'm sure you've got one too, because I know how the Enemy works. I pray that my testimony will encourage you not to let him stand in the way of your pursuing heaven's dream. Don't give in to the fear with which Satan seeks to control you. God has provided a way for us to tear down the stronghold of fear. The antidote is found in the apostle John's first epistle: "Where God's love is, there is no fear, because God's perfect love takes away fear. It is punishment that makes a person fear. So love is not made perfect in the person who has fear" (1 John 4:18 ICB).

From the Garden of Eden to the cross of Calvary, the Bible tells the story of God's unparalleled love. It loudly and completely answers questions first pondered in the Garden of Eden. There the devil raised doubt in human hearts and minds about God's goodness. He implied that God was withholding something wonderful from Adam and Eve and that they should step out and lay claim to that which God had forbidden. Once they questioned God's love, it was an easy next step for them to switch their allegiance. In one brief moment, Adam and Eve replaced the honor, esteem, and ardent devotion they'd felt toward God with honor and esteem for and ardent devotion to self. Outside the protective covering of God's love, they had become easy prey for their enemy, Satan.

Satan's Worst Nightmare

The only way back to freedom from fear is to finally be convinced that God's love is genuine, and that He deserves our honor, esteem, and ardent devotion. When we love and fear God, we will not fear man or Satan. Satan then loses control, and this is his worst nightmare. Remember that sin separates us from God. So without being able to motivate us through fear to sin, Satan is unable to keep us from the love of God, which dictates that we live the life He intended us to live from the beginning: "Loving means living the way he commanded us to live. And God's command is this: that you live a life of love. You have heard this command from the beginning" (2 John 1:6 ICB).

It was that love of God that conquered my fear and enabled me to stand before a crowd of people and present the gospel. And God's love is powerful enough to cancel your fear of anything else. The Bible says, "Whatever we do, it is because Christ's love controls us. Since we believe that Christ died for everyone, we also believe that we have all died to the old life we used to live. He died for everyone so that those who receive his new life will no longer live to please themselves. Instead, they will live to please Christ, who died and was raised for them" (2 Corinthians 5:14–15 NLT).

The love of God is powerful, and it takes power to deal with the devil, because he's not playing games. When the Bible says that he seeks to devour us, we must not take it lightly. The word *devour* brings stark clarity to what Satan wants to do to us. He wants to prey on us voraciously, to eat us up greedily, to consume us, to waste our lives, and ultimately to destroy us. The battle is real, the stakes are high, and the devil is in it to win.

Maybe he has already done a number on you, but if this book is still in your hands, he hasn't won the final battle.

When we come to understand that the original sin of Adam and Eve set us up to be focused on self rather than God, it helps us see that our own beliefs and ideas may be faulty. Satan capitalizes on this defective thinking by using the world around us to throw us off course. From the brainwashing messages of Madison Avenue to the secular viewpoint put forth on television, we're bombarded with demonic propaganda 24/7. The world is Satan's power base. Whether he's working to erode our moral fiber through socially acceptable evils or infiltrating our universities with the lie of evolution, the devil furtively slips into the hearts and minds of men and women to lead them astray and set them instead on paths that lead to destruction. His goal is to keep us from the truth of God that sets us free.

If we are to stand a chance at winning this battle, we need to immerse ourselves in the power base of God's truth—His Word. As we pursue heaven's dreams, knowing God's Word will be the difference between victory and defeat. The Scriptures are like radar for detecting Satan's lies. The Bible can name them, define them, and expose them. It's the compass that keeps us on course. This vital instrument becomes all the more crucial for our lives when we consider how far off course just one degree of variation can lead us.

> As we pursue heaven's dreams, knowing God's Word will be the difference between victory and defeat.

Allow me to illustrate. I own an ocean kayak. From where I launch on the Atlantic Ocean, I can make a two-mile journey to the nearest lighthouse or go south a mile to the nearest pier. Sometimes the wind blows hard or the current pulls strong, and if I'm not paying attention, I'll suddenly realize I've drifted. It happened one morning as I paddled out toward the lighthouse. I leaned back just for a few minutes to worship the Lord, and when I opened my eyes, I was drifting out to sea. What struck me about this experience was that I didn't do anything wrong; I simply didn't do anything. My nonaction became an action in the stream of those forces beyond my control.

I recently met with a man who hates exercise. He bought a treadmill and then sold it because he couldn't stand to use it. At the same time, he was deeply worried about his own mortality for the sake of his wife and young kids. I finally had to say to him, "What's more important to you, your family or your desire to be lazy? If you want to have more energy and give yourself a fighting chance to live longer, you're going to have to do something. Doing nothing is not an option."

Yet doing nothing that morning on my kayak trip was only part of the problem. Once I realized how far I had drifted, I froze. I became paralyzed with fear, which kept me going the wrong way even more. That's the power of fear—it stops us where we are and keeps us from moving toward our goal.

That's the Enemy's objective, to get us off course and then immobilize us and keep us from pursuing the dream God has for us. But God's Spirit is constantly calling us back to press on toward realizing our dreams.

Let's reflect and honestly assess our own lives. Have our dreams become unclear because we've allowed ourselves to drift off course spiritually? If we're going to stay the course, we'll need to be proactive about it. We must regularly exercise faith if we're to keep advancing in the right direction. Daily we must recalibrate our minds to counter the stream of negative, destructive, and deadly misinformation we will encounter throughout the day. The Bible warns us, "Don't copy the behavior and customs of this world, but let God transform you into a new person by changing the way you think. Then you will know what God wants you to do, and you will know how good and pleasing and perfect his will really is" (Romans 12:2 NLT).

The way God changes our thinking is through His Word: "All Scripture is given by God and is useful for teaching and for showing people what is wrong in their lives. It is useful for correcting faults and teaching how to live right. Using the Scriptures, the person who serves God will be ready and will have everything he needs to do every good work" (2 Timothy 3:16–17 ICB).

Jesus demonstrated how critical the knowledge of God's Word is. With the Word of God, Christ refuted every temptation the devil threw at Him in the wilderness (Luke 4:1–13). Since Jesus wasn't into formulas, this is noteworthy. He worked miracles in many different ways, perhaps so we wouldn't try to come up with a neat little template for healing the blind or raising the dead. Yet when He was tempted by Satan, Jesus used only one method of dealing with it—the Word of God.

Christ's consistent way of dealing with Satan's temptation shows us that our power base must also be God's Word. We cannot rely on our feelings, our own ideas, or anything else apart from the Scriptures.

Some of you may be realizing now how important a Bible-believing, Bible-teaching church can be to this critical battle. I know this can be a touchy subject since there are so many "bad" churches out there. But regardless of whatever disastrous experiences we've had with inadequate churches, God still wants believers to gather together: "Pursue faith and love and peace, and enjoy the companionship of those who call on the Lord with pure hearts" (2 Timothy 2:22 NLT).

Jesus's final prayer before He left this earth was that believers would be unified. Unity in the body of Christ provides protection from Satan and his demonic forces.

Solomon, the wisest man who ever lived, put it this way:

Two people can accomplish more than twice as much as one; they get a better return for their labor. If one person falls, the other can reach out and help. But people who are alone when they fall are in real trouble. And on a cold night, two under the same blanket can gain warmth from each other. But how can one be warm alone? A person standing alone can be attacked and defeated, but two can stand back-to-back and conquer. Three are even better, for a triple-braided cord is not easily broken. (Ecclesiastes 4:9–12 NLT)

Our chances of withstanding the attacks of our enemy are so much better when we stand with others. I find it more than a coincidence that the Bible often uses the metaphor of sheep when it speaks of God's people. The parallels are endless, but one particular aspect is quite pertinent to this point. When wolves hunt sheep, their strategy is remarkable. They don't just jump on the flock and have a field day with as many sheep as they can take down. That's too risky because of the shepherd. Instead, the whole pack of wolves runs alongside the flock until a wolf can get one sheep to start looking at him instead of at the shepherd. Once a sheep has changed its focus, it slowly begins to move away from the other sheep and the protection of the shepherd. Because the sheep has its eyes on the wolf, it fails to notice that it is being drawn away from the flock. When that sheep is far enough away from the rest of the flock, the remaining wolves join the lone wolf who has drawn out the sheep for the kill.

A. W. Tozer, in his book *Born after Midnight*, captures the heart of this tragic illustration and shows us the importance of keeping our eyes on Jesus:

> The scriptural way to see things is to set the Lord always before us, put Christ in the center of our vision, and if Satan is lurking around, he will appear on the margin only and be seen as but a shadow on the edge of the brightness. It is always wrong to reverse this—to set Satan in the focus of our vision and push God out to the margin. Nothing but tragedy can come of such inversion.
>
> The best way to keep the enemy out is to keep Christ in. The sheep need not be terrified by the wolf; they have but to stay close to the shepherd. It is not the praying sheep Satan fears but the presence of the shepherd.
>
> The instructed Christian whose faculties have been developed by the Word and the Spirit will not fear the devil. When necessary, he will stand against the powers of darkness and overcome them by the blood of the Lamb and the word of his testimony. He will recognize the peril in which he lives and will know what to do about

it, but he will practice the presence of God and never allow himself to become devil-conscious.[2]

I conclude with this thought from Tozer because as we explore Satan's strategy in greater detail in the next chapter, I don't want you to become "devil-conscious." The devil is a powerful foe—too powerful for us to withstand in our own strength. Yet in Christ he has already been defeated. His tactics are really only smoke and mirrors to the man or woman who sees the battle through an eternal perspective that keeps its focus on the Good Shepherd—Jesus.

the *pit*

Joseph found himself in a pit—the place where dreams often die. It wasn't something he had planned on either. He was simply sent out by his father to check on the welfare of his brothers. Imagine the emotional terror of this teenage boy when he fell into the hands of his unscrupulous siblings. Although Joseph probably knew that his brothers were jealous of him, he surely never imagined the extent of their envy. As he approached them, he probably was prepared for the usual less-than-warm greeting but not for the hostile reception he encountered. Certainly he had no idea that his life was on the line.

Instead of the customary mocking and callous interaction, he was seized, stripped of the garment that signified his father's favor, and thrown into a deep, dark, small place that offered no hope of escape. How apropos that this is the definition of a pit—a place that's deep, dark, small, and seemingly impossible to get out of. We've all had "pit" experiences, those miserable, depressing situations where there's no way out—at least not from a human perspective.

I think Moses must have felt the emotional horror of a pit experience when he heard Pharaoh say, "Yeah, well who is your God anyway?"

Noah probably understood that "pit" feeling, too, as he endured 120 years of ridicule—right up until it rained. Even Elijah found himself drowning in depression when he heard Jezebel say, "By this time tomorrow I will kill you. I will kill you as you killed those prophets. If I don't succeed, may the gods punish me terribly" (1 Kings 19:2 ICB). All these individuals—and many more, right up to the present day—have had their hopes thrown into deep pits where the growing seeds of doubt could have made them question the viability of their dreams.

As Joseph languished at the bottom of his pit, he might have struggled with that same doubt: "Did I get this right or not? Maybe my dream was just a figment of my own imagination, and God wasn't really in it. If the dream was real, would I be rotting here in this pit? Why did I even dare to believe in that stupid dream anyway? Look where it got me!"

Accomplices to the Pit

If I could break into Joseph's thought process at that point, I'd say, "Not so fast, Joe. Let's remember that you're not in the pit because of your dream. You're in the pit because of your brothers."

I love the fact that Scripture doesn't candy coat reality. The foul intent of Joseph's brothers is quite clear: "When Joseph's brothers saw him coming, they recognized him in the distance and made plans to kill him. 'Here comes that dreamer!' they exclaimed. 'Come on, let's kill him and throw him into a deep pit. We can tell our father that a wild animal has eaten him. Then we'll see what becomes of all his dreams!'" (Genesis 37:18–20 NLT).

Satan's strategy plays out no differently in our lives today. This is exactly what the Enemy wants to do to us. He sarcastically and contemptuously taunts, "Oh, here comes the dreamer, Mr. Christian. What does he think he's going to do? Win the world to Christ?" In my case it was more like, "Oh, it's Bob. He's got a Bible. Does he think he's going to be some kind of Bible teacher or something?"

Now, of course, this isn't actually the devil himself getting in our faces. He and his demonic forces work in and through other people. It could be someone at work or at the gym. Satan will even use other Christians to toss us and our dreams into a pit.

Make no mistake: members of our spiritual family, who should be agents of encouragement and ministers of understanding, are often the most effective tools the devil can employ to deliver his potent darts of doubt and discouragement. Our brothers and sisters in Christ can succeed in discouraging us because they carry so much more clout than a stranger would. If we don't value the opinions of our critics, it's easy to dismiss them. But it's different with our friends. In fact, the higher the level of respect we hold for the people making the comments—the more we wish to please and be respected by them—the more devastating their blows.

> Make no mistake: members of our spiritual family are often the most effective tools the devil can employ to deliver his potent darts of doubt and discouragement.

"Pastor Bob," you might say, "would a believer really discourage another brother or sister that way? Would a believer actually say negative and discouraging things?" Not only can I confirm this, but I'll even give you an example from my own life how this can happen without the vessels of offense ever knowing that they've just done the devil's dirty work.

I had been a Christian for only a couple of months. One weekend our senior pastor challenged the congregation: "When you go out to lunch together, don't just talk about ball scores or the latest movie; talk about the Word. Bring your Bible into the restaurant, open it up, have a time of *koinonia*—deep spiritual fellowship."

I was still new enough in my faith that I would actually try to do what my pastor said. Just as a little side note: can I say that having been a pastor now for more than twenty years, I love that kind of fresh faith. Seeing the brash and bold faith of new believers in our congregation is part of what keeps my own faith alive and active. Quite frankly, I don't know how we ever get so "wise" that we quit taking the Word at face value, but somewhere between conversion and death it can happen to the best of us. That's why I recommend every seasoned saint take one of these precious new believers under his or her wing. Both will benefit tremendously from the mixture of fresh faith and aged wisdom.

So I listened to my pastor's challenge and thought, *What a great idea*. Later that day, after the church service, I was at a friend's house with a group of singles from the church. We had finished the meal and were hanging out, so I made a suggestion. "Hey, why don't we just open up the Bible. I'll read a verse and make a short comment, and we can all talk about verses." (I remind you that these were friends.)

My buddy turned to me and said, "Who's going to teach us?"

"Well, I don't know that anyone will really teach us," I responded, "but let's just talk about the Bible."

Then another friend looked at me and said, in a somewhat sarcastic tone, "Oh, are you going to lead us in a Bible study? Who do you think you are—*Pastor* Bob?"

In hindsight I find this somewhat humorous, maybe even prophetic, but I didn't think it was too funny at the time. It wasn't like I was pushing myself into the position, but I did realize that something was happening in my heart. I wanted to see Christians get into the Word of God, and the devil was right there to make sure my enthusiasm and emerging dream got thrown into a pit pretty quickly.

I think it was because of this experience that even at an early stage in my Christian walk, I realized that certain people—even brothers and sisters in Christ—will discard our dreams and leave us in a pit. What

I've learned since then is that the real dream buster is not the flesh-and-blood person making the comments. It's the snake behind the scene that wants to replace our dreams with doubt.

I find it disconcerting that dreams are destroyed right here in the church on a regular basis. It happens each week after the altar call. People will hear the Bible study, the worship will inspire them, the Word will convict them, and they'll come forward to open their hearts to Christ. They make a profession of faith that goes something like this: "Yes, Jesus, I believe Your Word is true. I want to follow You. Today my life is Yours." Then, because they came with a friend who did not make that same statement of faith, it becomes an awkward moment in the car on the way home. As I've been told many times, the conversation goes something like this:

"So, uh, you opened up your heart and walked forward after that guy told everyone to get saved?"

"Let me tell you something. It was just so real. It was like God was actually speaking to me. I know the guy doesn't read my mail, but it was like he was talking directly to me."

With a bit more skepticism, the friend replies, "So you felt something, is that what happened? You went forward based on feeling rather than fact? What's the matter with you? It was an emotional moment. The guy worked you."

"I don't think he worked me."

"Well, he did. He does that every week. That's OK. I understand. Lots of people fall for it."

The person looks up defensively and says, "What do you mean, 'fall for'?"

Then, appealing to the person's pride, the friend says, "Well, you've never studied the Bible, have you? Did you know it's filled with contradictions?"

"Contradictions? I had no idea. Where are they?"

A bit more hostile the friend yells, "Everyone says it's filled with contradictions. I don't know exactly where, but they're there. Just trust me on this one. Besides, if you get serious about this religion thing, what do you think is going to happen to all your relationships?"

> We actually have the ability to speak life or death into the lives of those around us.

"What do you mean? What's going to happen to my relationships?"

And then the devil, through this unwitting but willing pawn, moves in for the kill: "How long have you and Sally been dating? Aren't you getting close? Isn't she talking about moving in? Well, you can't move in with her now. That church isn't going to be OK with that. They don't want anyone living together. That's their head trip."

Despondent but resolved, the person replies, "Well, maybe I can talk to Sally."

The friend raises another doubt as quickly as the first: "And what about your boss? You think the sales staff is going to welcome Mr. Honest Bible Thumper who's trying to sell things he knows don't have as much value as he's claiming?"

Finally the person falters under the attack. "So in other words, I was moved by feeling, the Bible is a book filled with contradictions, I'm going to lose my girlfriend, and I'll probably lose my job. Is that what you're saying?"

Satisfied, the friend emphatically says, "Yeah! You'd better think this through again."

"All right, maybe you are right. Maybe the whole thing was just a figment of my emotional imagination."

Within a matter of minutes, another dream ends up in the pit.

That's how powerful the influence of a friend can be. It's no wonder the Bible tells us to choose our friends wisely: "The righteous should choose his friends carefully, for the way of the wicked leads them astray" (Proverbs 12:26).

One of the reasons we have such a radical impact upon one another is because of the power of our words: "The tongue has the power of life and death" (Proverbs 18:21 NIV). We actually have the ability to speak life or death into the lives of those around us, just like in the illustration above. My words had spoken life, but the words of the friend spoke death.

As Christians our tongues should be used only to bring life: "Do not let any unwholesome talk come out of your mouths, but only what is helpful for building others up according to their needs, that it may benefit those who listen" (Ephesians 4:29 NIV). Encouragement has tremendous strength. That's one of the main reasons why the Bible is so emphatic about believers getting together: "Pursue righteousness, faith, love, peace with those who call on the Lord out of a pure heart" (2 Timothy 2:22). God expects us to come together for the purpose of pursuing righteousness, faith, love, and peace. We are supposed to support one another in our quest to know and love God, which includes encouraging and supporting one another as we pursue our God-given dreams.

So if brothers and sisters are supposed to be agents of encouragement, why do they so often become agents of discouragement instead? Jesus pegged it when He said that a prophet has no honor in his hometown (see Matthew 13:57). Knowing the human heart, He understood how hard it would be for those closest to us to actually believe that God would or could use us. Let's think about this soberly for a moment without letting our feelings get in the way.

If we're completely honest and don't suffer from massive pride, we're the first ones to be truly shocked when God uses us, and for the very same reasons our family is. We know ourselves—even better than they do—and we have a hard time believing that God could possibly make anything good come out of the wreckage of our lives.

Faith in the Pit

The "Have I really been chosen?" question will be one of the greater obstacles we face when we're in the pit. If the dream were valid, why would we be in a pit? But through the miracle of faith, God grants us the grace to believe that He actually can use us.

The thing to remember is, God gives the faith to *us*—not necessarily to our family and friends. So sometimes they'll look on and say, "It's nice you had a dream, but I know who you really are." Well, we know who we are too. But we have the accompanying faith to embrace our dreams and carry out what God has called us to do. Those who look on are not only surprised by God's choice, but they also lack the same measure of faith God has given to us. That's why they can be ready agents for the devil to discourage us and sabotage our dreams.

Although I can rationally see how this happens, it always grieves me when I witness Christians being used by the Enemy to discourage other believers. "Critics for Christ" seems to be a not-for-profit organization with a chapter in every church, complete with scheduled meetings, club members, and lobbyists. And when Satan finds a person with a dream, he quickly dispatches an agent of doubt—one of those angels of light we talked about in the last chapter. They're sent from hell with a question or criticism of our dream, and too often they find vessels through whom they can operate right in the midst of our closest friends.

Whenever I see this bad behavior among believers, I think back to that night in my friend's apartment and how painful it was to meet discouragement from those who were supposed to be supportive. Instead of encouraging someone's fresh faith, they failed to see the dream God was birthing in the heart of a baby believer.

I think that sense of frustration, disappointment, and discouragement could also be what Joseph felt at that moment when his brothers said, "Who are you? Do you think you're going to be in charge someday?" Joseph couldn't get them to see that it wasn't really he but rather God starting to work in and through him.

Prescription for the Pit

We can count on the fact that somewhere along the way, Satan will try to throw our dreams into the pit. And we can count on his trying to use those who are close to us to do it. So I want to offer a prescription for the pit. Proverbs 18:24 tells us, "A man who has friends must himself be friendly, but there is a friend who sticks closer than a brother." This verse helps us see that our way out of the pit is predicated upon God, not others. It gives us the hope that if our brothers and sisters let us down, if they throw our dreams and even us into a pit, we can still take heart. We have a Friend who sticks closer than a brother, and that Friend has other friends who will often come alongside at the exact moment of need.

Not every person in the body of Christ is susceptible to Satan's tactics in this area. Some believers are strong and courageous, pursuing their dreams, and fighting the battle successfully. God often uses such people to come alongside us at just the right time to pull us out of the pit. If we are to be successful in our pit experience, we must look to the Lord for our way out—by whatever means and vessel He chooses, no matter how illogical they may seem.

Every pit has an opening at the top. That's how we got in, and it's the only way we're likely to get out. Somebody put us there, and speaking in faith, somebody will pull us out. We see this illustrated in the life of Jeremiah.

The prophet was tossed into a pit because the princes of Israel didn't like what he had to say. Through divine intervention, however, an Ethiopian eunuch got word that Jeremiah was in a pit and petitioned the king for his release. The eunuch was given permission and thirty men to lift Jeremiah from the dark, vile, muddy pit:

Ebed-Melech went out of the king's house and spoke to the king, saying: "My lord the king, these men have done evil in all that they have done to Jeremiah the prophet, whom they have cast into the dungeon, and he is likely to die from hunger in the place where he is. For there is no more bread in the city." Then the king commanded Ebed-Melech the Ethiopian, saying, "Take from here thirty men with you, and lift Jeremiah the prophet out of the dungeon before he dies." So Ebed-Melech took the men with him and went into the house of the king under the treasury, and took from there old clothes and old rags, and let them down by ropes into the dungeon to Jeremiah. Then Ebed-Melech the Ethiopian said to Jeremiah, "Please put these old clothes and rags under your armpits, under the ropes." And Jeremiah did so. So they pulled Jeremiah up with ropes and lifted him out of the dungeon. And Jeremiah remained in the court of the prison. (Jeremiah 38:8–13)

Let's focus our attention on the "old clothes and rags" in this divine intervention. The King James Version is a bit more graphic: "old cast clouts and old rotten rags." These men came to Jeremiah and offered him dirty rags as a way of escape.

Jeremiah could have refused on the basis that this was just not the way he expected to be rescued. He could have insisted on certain parameters and conditions, but if he had, the book of Jeremiah would have ended in chapter 38, and the prophet would have died in the pit. Jeremiah had to be willing for his rescue from the pit to come through whatever means God chose. This required humility on the part of the prophet and a willingness to give up his own idea of how he should get out of the pit.

The Purpose of the Pit

Many times we find ourselves in a pit for one reason—we are in dire need of purification. Purity is a condition marked by the absence of additives. Through our pit experiences, God may be seeking to rid us of every hope for our dream that is not anchored in Him alone.

The Bible says, "When you ask God, you must believe. Do not doubt God. Anyone who doubts is like a wave in the sea. The wind blows the wave up and down. He who doubts is thinking two different things at the same time. He cannot decide about anything he does. A person like that should not think that he will receive anything from the Lord" (James 1:6–8 ICB).

We cannot maintain two different ways of thinking about our dreams. We either believe God is giving the dreams to us or we don't. God would prefer that we settle this matter once and for all and quit going back and forth—believing Him one minute and not believing Him the next, depending on our circumstances.

One reason for our double-mindedness is pride. Let me explain. We don't have to go to the pit; God gives us the option of purifying our own hearts: "Draw near to God and He will draw near to you. Cleanse your hands, you sinners; and purify your hearts, you double-minded" (James 4:8). God knows pride is a common yet dangerous response to being given a dream. The very fact that God chose Joseph was enough to make Joseph's head swell, but adding his youth and inexperience into the equation, we can see how difficult it would have been for Joseph to keep his heart pure and his ego small.

So the purpose of the pit is to purify our focus on God's glory alone, because that's the only way the dream can be accomplished. If we make the mistake of believing we're special and that's why God chose us, we may also believe we can make the dream happen on our own. Yet when circumstances throw up a roadblock or turn our comfortable expectations upside down, our self-assurance wanes. We find ourselves filled with doubt because we really aren't sufficient in ourselves to make the dream happen. But when we're anchored in the reality that our dream is God-given and can only be accomplished by Him, we'll give up our self-driven efforts—and our doubts.

I've often wondered how Joseph initially shared his dream with his brothers. Was it with a sense of amazement or with an attitude of arrogance?

Was it with passion or with pride? Proverbs 16:18 says, "Pride goes before destruction, and a haughty spirit before a fall." There's a better way to communicate a precious dream.

Most of us are familiar with the speech for which Martin Luther King Jr. is famous, in which he professed, "I have a dream." We've heard the tone of his voice and sensed the passion in his heart, without any trace of arrogance or pride. That's the proper way to communicate our dreams to others, but until our dreams have been stripped of every ounce of self-contamination, we won't be able to draw others into the excitement and sense of possibility.

In the pit Joseph was left alone with his dream. In the darkness and hopelessness of the pit, perhaps it began to dawn on him that his dream could not be realized through his own efforts—that it would only come about through supernatural intervention. In the pit all of Joseph's self-centered hopes of pulling off the dream himself had to die. And in the pit, he had to surrender his will to the will of the Dream Giver.

At the very moment our self-driven dreams die, God supernaturally brings about our rescue from the pit. The real test of whether the purification process is complete is in our response to God's method of rescuing us.

In the same way that Jeremiah did not refuse the rotten rags, so we, too, must not turn away from the means and method through which God chooses to pull us out of the pit. I have to believe that Joseph did not balk at how he got out. While I'm sure that the lessons of the pit continued long after he was pulled up from that dark little hole, I also have to believe that he was at least a bit more humble and circumspect in the way he shared his dream after the pit. No more cocky attitude and lack of consideration toward those with whom he was sharing. Had he thought even for a moment about how his dream might make others feel, he might have chosen his words more carefully. There is a way to share a dream that bypasses the pit and inspires those around to jump on our bandwagon. Martin Luther King Jr. knew that more excellent way, and the pit laid the groundwork for Joseph's understanding of that more excellent way as well.

> In the same way that Jeremiah did not refuse the rotten rags, so we, too, must not turn away from the means and method through which God chooses to pull us out of the pit.

We can usually spot someone who has fallen into this pitfall of pride. I recently had the opportunity to attend a luncheon with some other pastors. I turned to the man sitting next to me and asked him how things were going. He said, "Incredible! I'm conquering the world; going beyond; doing great things for God!" I was so dumbfounded by his arrogance that I truly found myself speechless—a condition that's rare for me. I got the distinct impression that this man really felt he could take on the world by himself for God. I had no inspiration to get on board and help. Instead, I was a bit turned off by his boastful response.

Pit experiences tend to destroy the pride in us. They also tend to cleanse that putrid part of our hearts that has the audacity to think that God got a good deal when He saved us. I'm so glad Joseph had his pit experience, because without the purification process, his dream never could have been accomplished. He never would have been humble enough to recognize God's divine hand through his circumstances.

The lessons of Joseph, Moses, and others make me stop and reflect about God's supernatural work through the natural course of my life. Even when I'm criticized by my brothers and sisters in Christ, I've learned that I can still hear God's voice guiding and directing me. In fact, over the years I've come to see that every criticism is an opportunity to learn and grow.

It used to be that when someone would complain and then add, "Oh, you just have such a big church, I guess you can't help it if someone slips through the cracks," I would get defensive. I believe the size of our church actually makes us try harder. So in my frustration, I tended to ignore such complaints. Over time, however, I started to rethink my reaction and began to consider that what people might be saying is, "I need a sense of community. What are you doing to help me feel like I belong?"

It was this criticism that led our pastoral team to make certain decisions that, I believe, transformed our church into a place where people can find that sense of community. That valuable change never would have occurred if I had continued to let the criticisms of others discourage me to the point of inaction. I would have missed the whole point of why I was being challenged in the first place.

God always wants to make our dreams bigger and better, but that requires from each of us a surrendered life and a heart that doesn't question the means by which God chooses to orchestrate our dreams. It also takes humility and a willingness to acknowledge that the enormity of the task is well beyond our own individual abilities. God designed it that way because He wants us to trust and rely on Him.

The Providence of the Pit

Whatever our dreams, in time we'll most likely find that parts of them intertwine and overlap with the dreams of others. In fact, the bigger the dream, the more parties it may take to accomplish it. The pit experience purifies us to be open to this team concept.

Note how Jesus prayed: "Father, I pray that all people who believe in me can be one. You are in me and I am in you. I pray that these people can also be one in us, so that the world will believe that you sent me" (John 17:21 ICB).

God's heart for unity is a resounding theme throughout Scripture, so why would it strike us as odd that He wants this unity when it comes to fulfilling our dreams? Almost no accomplishment of a grand magnitude is a solo effort. Even now I'm thinking of two people who are laboring with me on this book to make my dream of sharing truth with others a reality. They, too, have been given dreams by God, and some of those dreams complement my own. In our joint effort, I contribute the bone and marrow, and they put on the muscle and sinew. Together we do what none of us could do alone.

Other people are being prepared by God to assist us with our dreams because that's the way God orchestrates and coordinates His body. Think about all the things you, personally, have accomplished in your life and how God used others to come alongside you to help fulfill your dream. For fun, track the miracles of the Bible and see how many of them required the participation of more than just one individual.

That's why when we share our dreams with arrogance, pride, and self-centeredness, in an attitude of "I don't need anybody else to make my dream happen," we could very well be alienating the people God has chosen to help us. If we approach our dreams this way, we shouldn't be surprised when we end up in a pit for a time of purification.

If you're in the pit with your dream right now, I hope you've felt the encouragement of this chapter. The pit is not a time for us to be pitiful;

it's a time for us to be purified. God wants to get rid of the dross of pride in our hearts so we'll share heaven's dreams for our lives with the passion that attracts others like a magnet.

The Enemy's tactic is to stoke our pride and isolate us, like the wolf that draws the sheep away from the flock. God's solution is for us to get together with other brothers and sisters—those who have pure hearts, who are not double-minded but fixed upon God—and let their fire and enthusiasm energize our dreams.

Perhaps this book is what God designed to pull you out of your pit. You have a choice at this point. You can put the book down, return to your "pit-y" party and say, "That's not how I'm going to get out of this pit!" Or you can use the ropes of encouragement and truth in these pages to pull yourself out of the pit. It's your choice, but you should know that we're only halfway through the journey toward our dreamality. Once we're out of the pit, we will have a few more obstacles to overcome. The good news is that God awaits us at our very next scrimmage with Satan.

the *marketplace*

Have you ever invented something in your mind? Ever lounged in bed and entertained a thought, considered a concept, given birth to a brain-child? I have—a million times. Some ideas are brilliant, if I do say so myself. Others are just practical. It wasn't that long ago that I was thinking about those water pitchers that waiters carry in restaurants. I can't help holding my breath when they walk up to the table, take a glass, and try to fill it. Will the ice in that pitcher, caught between the rim and the building pressure of the water, suddenly give way and send water and ice sloshing onto the table—or my lap?

So one morning I thought, *They need to do something about that!* I even devised a solution to the problem. But just last week, I was at a restaurant when the waiter approached the table with a pitcher that had funnels on three sides and a trap on the inside to hold back the ice. It was the perfect solution to the problem I'd been pondering. One might think that the sight of this new pitcher would have delighted me—that I would have been happy about it. Quite the contrary, I was actually a bit taken aback and bothered. I even had a tinge of regret because I felt like I'd been ripped off. Someone had taken my idea!

It happens to all of us. My wife came up with an idea for heated windshield wipers for winter: at the press of a button, the wipers would heat up and melt the ice off the windshield. She was disappointed when she discovered someone had already had her idea, manufactured it, and was probably making a bundle from it.

From water pitchers to heated windshield wipers and everything in between, we all have experienced that hopeful moment when something is right there on our horizon. We can almost feel it in our grasp. Our hearts race, our hopes rise, and our sense of possibility awakens—then all of a sudden the big dream vanishes before our very eyes. Gone. Disappeared without recourse. Permanently wiped out of the realm of possibility. We have entered the nightmare zone, and this is another of Satan's tactics to keep us from making heaven's dreams our realities.

Dreams for Sale

Before we have a chance to rejoice in our dreams, the devil launches what I call a "sale of our dream" attack. It's the one he likes to wage against us right after we've been dragged out of the pit. That was Satan's next tactical maneuver against Joseph.

Joseph's brothers plotted to kill him by throwing him in the pit. Through a sudden change of heart, they decided not to kill him but to use him for profit instead: "Judah said to his brothers, 'What profit is there if we kill our brother and conceal his blood? Come and let us sell him to the Ishmaelites, and let not our hand be upon him, for he is our brother and our flesh.' And his brothers listened" (Genesis 37:26–27). They determined that killing their brother would benefit them less than selling him.

When we have great dreams or ideas, others may try to kill them. But once they realize that our dreams have value, they'll be quick to exploit them for their own gain. Joseph's brothers realized that as long as Joseph was in the picture, they would always take second place in their father's heart. Joseph's dream reinforced that. But as they plotted to kill him, it dawned on them that they could double their benefit by keeping him alive. If they sold him into slavery, not only would the position of favor be up for grabs, but they could make a bit of money, as well.

I can't help but make a quick commentary on this area of Scripture. I hope I don't offend anyone, but I have a sense of humor that just can't pass these verses by without noting the hilarity of Judah's remark. The scene plays out in my mind like this: Here's a bunch of brothers who ask themselves, "What should we do with our brother?" Then they decide, "Well, let's kill him." But one of the brothers comes up with a bright idea—"No, let's not kill him. He's our brother. Let's sell him." *Hello!* We need brothers like this, right? "Let's not kill him and have blood on our hands; let's just sell the guy." That's what we should do to our brother?

If we just read the text and take it at face value, we might chuckle at the brothers' line of thinking. But it stops being funny when we realize that this is exactly how the Enemy works. He tries to make us think that our dreams are negotiable: if we can't or won't do them, someone else can and will. The Enemy often employs our brothers and sisters to accomplish this demonic ploy. We think someone else is about to live out our dreams because we see our dreams taking shape in that person's life. We may even protest, "Hey! That was my idea." Or, "I proposed that to the boss first. It wasn't even his idea, but now he gets all the credit!"

Satan has spent countless years observing mankind, and he can read us well. Knowing my fears and hesitations, many times he has stood right in my face and yelled, "Bob's dreams are for sale. Anyone want to act on Bob's dreams? Bob will never step out in faith to see his dreams fulfilled, but if you'd like to have Bob's dreams, just place your bid." I've even objected, "My dreams are not for sale. How can you say my dreams are for sale?" But because I become immobilized by fear, suddenly it appears that my dreams may be up for sale. Someone else may have the courage and faith to step out and do what I can't seem to bring myself to accomplish. How much money could I have made on the innovative pitcher that someone else designed first because all I did was think about it? What if my wife had patented her design for windshield wipers instead of just talking about it?

I remember the first time we considered holding our Easter service at a local baseball stadium. Our church attendance was running around three thousand, and the stadium had a capacity of ten thousand. I agonized over whether to take the step of faith required to pull off an event of that magnitude. I knew that God's dream for my life was to preach the gospel to as many people as possible. I also knew this would be a glorious opportunity for evangelism, yet I was gripped with fear.

Before coming to Christ, as I had mentioned earlier, I had suffered from agoraphobia. So as I thought of standing in front of thousands of people in a venue of that size, Satan went to work filling my head with thoughts like, *Who do you think you are? You're going to waste all that money, and no one will show up.* And when that didn't work, he started at the other end of the spectrum: *What if ten thousand people do show up? You'll have to speak in front of all of them!* The Enemy kept reminding me that I was no Billy Graham, a fact I knew well.

By God's grace alone, I did not give in to the fear that had once controlled my life. I did step out in faith and fulfill that part of God's dream for my life. That stadium event became the first of many. We now fill stadiums of 22,000 plus, and I preach the gospel to as many as God will bring.

What if I had given in to the fear? What if I had believed the lie of the Enemy that I couldn't do it? God surely would have raised up another person to fulfill His purpose, and I could have been left feeling like my dream was snatched out from under me.

Whenever we assume that our dreams have been put up for grabs and someone else is fulfilling our call in life, we can feel cheated. "God, why them and not me? I thought that was my dream, my plan, my hope, my . . . my mate." Sometimes it actually gets that serious. Like when you dated the same girl for four years and really believed she was the one for you. But the two of you had had so much conflict that you decided it was best to slow the relationship down. So you made the phone call: "I'm really sorry, but I think we should just put this thing on hold for a while."

She comes back with something you weren't ready for: "So it's OK for us to date others?"

"Well, sure, I guess so, if you want to. I don't know why you would even go there. We're just putting the relationship on hold for a while, but yeah, OK."

Six months pass. You talk from time to time, but now it looks like she's actually going out with someone else, and to make matters worse, you told her it was OK. You just didn't think she really would. Then you get the phone call you never expected: "Hi, you're never going to guess what's happening," she starts.

"What?" you ask curiously.

She continues, "You know how you said we should date other people? Well, I've been dating for a few months, and guess what? Last night he popped the question. He gave me a ring. I'm so glad you had the spiritual maturity to see that our relationship wasn't working out, or I never would have been available for this relationship. Oh, and by the way, you're invited to the wedding!"

You're on the other end of the line having a heart attack. Four months later you're at the wedding watching your girlfriend marry . . . your old friend? He was your roommate for how long? And now . . . *That's my girl. That was my dream. That was my plan.*

Can I highlight the obvious in this situation? Marrying that girl wasn't really your dream. That girl isn't your wife because she's the other guy's wife. I know that sounds simplistic and ridiculously apparent, but that's my point. Something is not a God-given dream if it isn't manifested in life. God-given dreams can't be bought or sold in the marketplace. He has plans for us that become our dreams, and because they're the dreams He has for us, He'll make sure they come to pass.

The Remedy for a Lost Dream

Still, losing a dream can be devastating and downright debilitating. It might be hard to believe that our dreams still exist when we see what we thought was God's plan go down the tubes for us and happen in someone else's life. It's difficult to handle the disappointment that results from a bursting bubble. And it will probably take a while to regroup after we watch what we thought was our God-given dream rides off in a white limousine with tin cans trailing.

The remedy for the heartbreak of a vanquished dream is to realize God's perfection. For all of us who have watched our dreams go up for sale, we need to remember that whatever does not occur in our lives is not really God's dreams for us. So if the dreams we've been holding on to never materialize, chances are they were self-driven.

But God does have a dream, a unique plan designed specifically for each of us. This understanding is the first step to recovery after we've been dragged through the marketplace of self-driven dreams.

God's Sovereignty on Display

Most times we find ourselves in that marketplace for the sole purpose of being shaken loose from the self-driven dreams we hold on to so tightly. God will actually allow us to witness the sale of a dream to which we've been clinging so He can prepare us to receive the one heaven has for us.

Often, in the wake of losing our dreams, we're left with great anxiety, a deep sense of frustration, even jealousy. I can't help but think that might have been how Joseph felt when this happened to him. Did he wonder, when he was in the pit, which brother might take his place in his father's heart? Did it ever cross his mind that perhaps God would use one of his siblings to fulfill the dream instead of him?

We have an advantage Joseph didn't, in that we can step outside of any particular chapter of Genesis and consider the entire narrative. The story of Joseph's life doesn't conclude until chapter 50. In the end we can see that Joseph's dream was never on the line. He may have been sold, but his dream was never for sale.

> God does have a dream, a unique plan designed specifically for each of us.

Joseph's story has a happy ending, but he didn't know that when his brothers turned on him. All he knew was that it seemed his dream might be taken away. That's the deception of the marketplace. The devil keeps us in that nightmarish place of the unknown, where he works us over with doubt and confusion. Joseph languished in a pit while his brothers deliberated over whether to kill him or sell him. As we know, they decided it was better to sell him to a band of Midianites whose destination was Egypt.

In the greater picture of what would happen in Joseph's life, being sold to the Midianites was an integral step in God's plan for Joseph's life. In fact, it is profound—we can see the sovereignty and providence of God in action.

Just as the pit serves the purpose of purifying us, so the apparent loss of our dreams is also designed with an objective in mind. The refining that takes place when we think our dreams may be up for grabs perfects our knowledge of God. And that refining is the remedy. The pit purifies our sight so we can see that the dream is God's dream in the first place and that if it is to be fulfilled, God will have to do it—it's beyond our reach. But the marketplace of dreams is designed to help us see God's ability to fulfill that dream.

The Bible tells us that God "opens doors, and no one can shut them; he shuts doors, and no one can open them" (Revelation 3:7 NLT). God is the one who runs the universe. Grasping this concept of His sovereignty is paramount to having victory over this deception of the marketplace. That's why we need to spend a bit more time looking long and hard at God's absolute control.

God's Omniscience

God is omniscient, or all-knowing: "Our Lord is great and very power-ful. There is no limit to what he knows" (Psalm 147:5 ICB). If God were not all-knowing, if there were even one thing that God didn't know, then He could not be sovereign. That lack of information would keep Him from being able to rule everything from a position of total understanding. Without the knowledge of even one minor fact, He would not be able to have total control.

It's a bit like our lack of control because of our limited knowledge of the weather. We can't control or even accurately predict what the weather will be. Our plans are subject to change because of something as simple as the weather.

God's omniscience means He's never surprised—by the weather or by anything we humans do. That should bring us great comfort when we sin. God knows even our smallest sins, but He loves us anyway.

Remember how great you felt the day He saved you? Remember feeling His absolute, all-encompassing love and the security of His sal-vation? God knew then that you would fail. If you could believe He loved you then, believe it now, because He knew everything about you then. God's love and salvation are made perfect by His omniscience.

God's Omnipotence

God is also omnipotent, or all-powerful. Again Scripture offers confirmation: "For with God nothing will be impossible" (Luke 1:37); "All power is his forever and ever." (1 Peter 5:11 NLT). Even one stray atom of power that belonged to someone else would be sufficient to conflict with God's absolute control. It would make Him a limited ruler and unable to do exactly what He determined to do in His omniscience. God delegates His authority to others (see Romans 13:1), but it is completely and totally His and can be given and withdrawn at His will.

God's Freedom

God's sovereignty requires that He be absolutely free to do whatever He wills anywhere, at any time. Ephesians 1:11 tells us, "God is the One who makes everything agree with what he decides and wants" (ICB). Romans 11:34–36 says, "Who can know what the Lord is thinking? Who knows enough to be his counselor? And who could ever give him so much that he would have to pay it back? For everything comes from him; everything exists by his power and is intended for his glory" (NLT).

Our understanding of freedom is limited because nothing on earth is absolutely free. Everything is interdependent and subject to all the physical and spiritual laws put into place by God. We've all heard the phrase "free as a bird," yet a bird is subject to the weather, the food supply, instincts, and predators. That's not exactly free.

Our freedom will always be limited, but God enjoys absolute freedom because nothing can hinder Him, compel Him, or stop Him. Because He is all-powerful and all-knowing, He's able to do as He pleases always, everywhere, and forever.

God's Majesty

God is so far beyond our comprehension that it's hard to fathom His majesty and impossible to grasp Him totally. Just for fun, let's get a little perspective on the grandeur of God from a scientific viewpoint.

The size of the universe is astounding to ponder. To simply look at the night sky and consider the impressive power it took to create it all has undoubtedly boosted the faith of stargazers ever since Adam first looked into the heavens. But consider what we know today. When we look into the night sky, we're not seeing just stars and planets. Some of those points of light are entire galaxies.

Our own galaxy, the Milky Way, is an average-sized system, yet it's one hundred thousand light-years in diameter and contains two hundred billion stars. Even if we were to count stars at a rate of three per second, in a hundred years we would have counted less than five percent of the stars in our galaxy![1]

Mind-boggling, isn't it? Now, in light of that, let's consider these scriptures:

- *"By faith we understand that the worlds were framed by the word of God, so that the things which are seen were not made of things which are visible." (Hebrews 11:3)*

- *"When I consider Your heavens, the work of Your fingers, the moon and the stars, which You have ordained, what is man that You are mindful of him, and the son of man that You visit him?" (Psalm 8:3–4)*

- *"Who has measured the waters in the hollow of his hand, or with the breadth of his hand marked off the heavens?" (Isaiah 40:12 NIV)*

God measures with His hand what we cannot even imagine or fathom with our entire being. God is not just a superhuman. He's altogether out of our league.

God's Providence

It's this all-knowing, all-powerful, totally free, sovereign God who planned and is now orchestrating the details of our dreams. He has a definitive plan for each one of us: "'I know the plans I have for you,' declares the LORD, 'plans to prosper you and not to harm you, plans to give you hope and a future'" (Jeremiah 29:11 NIV).

This may seem weird, but stay with me for a minute. Look closely at your index finger. That index finger is yours. I know—pretty obvious, and you wish I would get to the point that will make you say wow, but listen. The fact that your fingerprint is exclusively yours means no one else has that same print. You could go back in history to the beginning of mankind and into the future, all the way to the end of human existence, and find that no one else has had, does have, or ever will have your fingerprint. Now that's unique. But it's no more unique than God's plan for your life. Just as He made that print for you, He has made a plan for your life that's just for you. It's yours alone.

I hope this is sinking in. In order for us not to miss God's unique plan for our lives, we must make sure we're following the path of God's will for us. We've got to get our attention off what everyone else is doing with dreams we thought they stole. The only way to do this is to come to a more perfect—or mature—understanding of God's sovereignty. Our dreams cannot be stolen out from under us when God is in absolute control. Therefore, if our dreams seem to vanish, they weren't really God's dreams for us.

We can find perhaps no greater display of God's providence than in the story of Moses. As recorded in the book of Exodus, Pharaoh had decreed that all the male children born to the Israelites should be killed. To save the life of her infant son, Moses's mother put him into the Nile River in a little makeshift papyrus basket. Through the providential power of God, as Pharaoh's daughter was bathing, she discovered the basket with Moses in it. What were the chances of that little basket with the baby inside making it to a group of women in the river, and one of them just happening to be Pharaoh's daughter? Slim to none? Well, the story gets better.

Moses's sister was standing a small distance from the basket to see what would happen to Moses. When she saw Pharaoh's daughter pull him from the river, she offered Moses's mother as a nursemaid for the baby. Moses's mom, in faith, released her child into God's care, and He divinely, sovereignly, and providentially orchestrated the child's rescue and return back into her care.

The skeptics among us might think, *Well, that's the Bible, and that was many years ago.* For a more modern example, let's consider this true story from one of our staff members at Calvary Chapel Fort Lauderdale:

I had walked past that storefront window countless times. There it was—a shiny, purple, and perfect new bicycle.

There are just some things that all children want, and I was no exception. "Oh, the things I could do with that beautiful new bike!" I thought.

My father was a pastor, and our family did not have a lot of money, so I decided to save my allowance and odd-job money to buy myself the bicycle. Every week I walked past the store to see "my" beautiful purple bike.

I worked hard to save my money and kept praying that God would bring me what I wanted.

One day during Sunday school, my teacher talked about a missionary family in need. She told us about the horrible sickness this family was enduring. Reading from a letter written by the family, she told the class about the little boy who had contracted hepatitis, most likely from a typhoid shot he had received in Chile. All week I thought about that little boy far away in Chile.

The next Sunday my teacher asked us what we should do to help this little boy. All the children decided he could really use a brand-new bike—that would cheer him up for sure! I remember my heart almost stopping. I said, "Oh no, God, not my bike!" But then I knew I had to give my bike money to my teacher so it could help that little boy in Chile get a bike.

One week later I gave my money to the teacher.

Many years later in college, I began praying that God would send me a godly husband.

My father was still a pastor and was also teaching at a local Baptist college. When I went home for Christmas vacation one year, I met Philip at my father's church. Philip was attending the Baptist college where my father taught. In fact, he was in his class.

Not long after my Christmas break I decided to transfer to this same college. I got to know Philip better since my college roommate was engaged to his best friend and my parents and Philip's parents were also friends.

Our first date was on Valentine's Day. It soon became obvious that we were made for each other. We decided to get married. I didn't know then just how God-ordained our relationship was.

One evening, after both our families had eaten dinner together, Philip's mom started reminiscing about their missionary days and what life was like on the field with small children. She shared about a time in Chile when the whole family had been terribly sick and how Philip had come down with hepatitis, presumably from a typhoid shot. I couldn't believe what I was hearing! My husband was the little boy that I had given up my bike money for! He was the very one that God had put on my heart to help! I had to leave the room because I was so emotional—I just could not stop crying.

God had been so good to me. My heart's desire was for a shiny, perfect, purple bicycle, but God had it in His heart to use that longing to give me much, much more—a godly husband that He had ordained from the very beginning.

Philip and I now have three grown children and have been married for twenty-nine years. We know in our hearts and hold on to the fact that God made us for each other and planned it that way before even time began.[2]

Clarification of the Dream

If our dreams really are divine dreams, one of the things that will happen during a time of testing, when it looks the most like someone has stolen our dreams, is that we'll realize no one has stolen anything from us. We'll start to see that our dreams are becoming more our dreams, and what we perceived to be taken from us was actually someone else's dream. God is merely perfecting our knowledge of His sovereignty while He streamlines and personalizes our dreams.

For several years we have been on local and national television. A few years ago, I wanted to change the style of our television show. I wanted to move away from the talking-head format and go to a "pod" layout. I felt this would be a better flow. We did a few shows, but for many reasons, we ended up going back to our old format.

Recently as I was flipping through the channels on my television, I saw T. D. Jakes, senior pastor of The Potter's House, a nondenominational megachurch in Dallas, Texas, doing the very thing I'd been trying to accomplish. I have to be honest and say that part of my heart sank in disappointment. I heard myself saying, "Aw, he's doing what I wanted to do!"

But he's not doing it exactly the same way I had envisioned. He didn't take my dream. He has his own dream that God is fulfilling through him. When God is ready, and if He's willing, by His providential hand and in His sovereign plan, my dream in this area will come to fruition. If it doesn't, then it wasn't my dream. I'm OK with that because I know that whenever the Lord takes away something I thought was going to be good, He gives back something much better. That's the beauty and benefit of His sovereignty.

Trusting the Sovereignty of God

In the marketplace of our dreams, we are perfecting our knowledge of the sovereignty of God in our lives. In the pit we realized that our dreams are not our own, but in the marketplace it begins to dawn on us that our lives are not really our own either. They belong to the almighty, all-knowing God who is the author of our dreams. Our knowledge of Him must be perfected if ever we are to trust in His ability to carry out our dreams and to do with our lives what is in our best interest. If we don't see Him as able, in control, and on our side, we will always be prone to second-guess what He's doing and try to take matters back into our own hands.

As I mentioned before, I have a few friends who are in professional sports. It's not uncommon for me to get a phone call from someone with whom I've been building a relationship to tell me that he has been traded. He'll have to move to another city, and it's questionable whether he will ever return to our church fellowship.

That happened recently with a hockey player I know. He received a call and was told that he was no longer a part of his current team but had been traded to another. That meant that he would have to give up his home, the friends he'd made in that area, and his ties with our church. He would have to move his kids to new schools and change almost every aspect of his life. His entire world would be altered by that decision. Obviously, he had the chance to decline the trade, against the judgment of his agent, but he didn't. Why? He knew that his agent was in control and was working for his best interest. Based on this assurance, he released and entrusted his prerogative to make the decision to his agent.

This example of trust is how the relationship is supposed to work between us and God. I could ask all kinds of questions when I look at the drawbacks of being senior pastor of a large ministry, like "Why am I in South Florida? Why didn't I get a more laid-back area like Costa Rica? Why did God pick me? Was I not at the right time in the right place?" I don't ask those questions, because I settled the underlying question years ago. God is my agent, and He has my best interest at heart. That means whatever decisions He makes about my life are fine with me, regardless of what they cost me, because He's only doing what's best for me.

I love Pastor Chuck Smith's teaching on the birth of Christ. We see that Joseph and Mary were living in Nazareth before Jesus was born, yet Scripture clearly teaches that Jesus was to be born in Bethlehem. Pastor Chuck says in his book *The Search for the Messiah*, "God is able to direct the decisions and the paths of kings and peasants in order to accomplish his will. So, Caesar Augustus made the decree that everyone should be taxed. Since Joseph and Mary were in the line of David, they were required to go to their family's town of origin, Bethlehem of Judea. No doubt Joseph and Mary marveled at the method God used to return them to Bethlehem and thus fulfill the prophecy."[3]

> We can only find peace in the out-of-control times if we understand that God is in control.

I love that! If it's God's dream, then it's His job to orchestrate and fulfill the details of the dream.

It doesn't take long in life for us to realize that we can control some things, but many others are totally out of our control. We can only find peace in the out-of-control times if we understand that God is in control. We have to remember that God is trying to perfect our understanding of His sovereignty. That's why He sometimes allows it to seem as though our dreams are going to someone else or in directions over which we have no control.

Perhaps Joseph had the sinking feeling that his dream, which had seemed so vibrant when God first gave it to him, had faded to a dull memory of what might have been had his life not undergone such a drastic change. But if he looked at the appearance of the Midianites—the guys who bought him—in light of God's sovereignty, he might have recognized God's hand moving behind the scenes, orchestrating events according to His divine timing. Each little piece of the puzzle of Joseph's life was being put into place.

In the pit Joseph began to understand that his dream was really God's dream in the first place, and without God he couldn't realize the dream. Then in the marketplace, where dreams appear to be negotiable, he learned that God is supremely qualified to seal the promise of our dreams. Rather than being left to die in a pit, God sovereignly plucked Joseph from the jaws of death and placed him in the hands of envoys who would deliver him to just the right place at just the right time—not to his final destination, but to an important point along the path. For us the lesson is that the closer we get to resting in God, the more opportunity we'll have to see His perfect plan.

How intricate is God's involvement in our dreams? The Bible says, "In Him we live and move and have our being" (Acts 17:28). Stop for a moment and ask yourself this question: How are you breathing right now? Are you making yourself breathe? No. In healthy people, breathing is one of many natural processes that occur with no need for us to consciously be involved. Whether it's our lungs breathing, our hearts beating, our livers filtering, our blood cells regenerating, or any of the other millions of functions that go on without our attention, the source of our lives is not us but God. The same God who authorizes and orchestrates every breath we take is the same God who has providentially prepared a path for each of us.

But the Bible also tells us that we are co-laborers with Him (see Colossians 1:29). Sometimes God simply does a work in us, but other times we need to step out in the faith He gives us. The apostle Paul wrote, "By the grace of God I am what I am, and His grace toward me was not in vain; but I labored more abundantly than they all, yet not I, but the grace of God which was with me" (1 Corinthians 15:10). Paul participated in God's plan for him. If he had refused the grace of God, nothing would have been accomplished. Likewise, there are times we must choose to walk forward in the dreams God has given us. The question is when. It's in this critical decision about timing that the perfection process of the marketplace has the greatest impact. It helps us to see the importance of proceeding according to God's timing.

Some of what happens while we wait on God's timing is that He works in the lives of others who will eventually be part of what He's doing in our lives. He prepares them so that by the time we get to the appropriate stage of the journey, we can connect with the person or people God has foreordained to complement our dream. It's a glorious moment when all parties recognize the sovereignty and providence of God in bringing our lives together for that divine appointment.

When that happens, we stop stressing over the missed appointment, tomorrow's meetings, our dead-end jobs, or our situations in life. We begin to trust that where we are now, the conversations we're having, the things we're doing, and the people we're meeting are the right places, the right opportunities, the right actions, and the right connections because God is orchestrating our lives.

King Solomon, who is known for his wisdom, said, "There is a right time for everything. Everything on earth has its special season" (Ecclesiastes 3:1 ICB). When I search for the word *time* in the Bible software I use, I see that it appears more than six hundred times in the New King James Version. Although God lives outside of time and space, He created time, and He's acutely aware of the importance of timing. So is Satan. The devil knows that it's in this arena of timing that he can frustrate, anger, humiliate, and discourage us if we don't have a firm belief in God's sovereignty. The Enemy will whisper, "It's not happening yet. It's not happening now. It's never going to happen."

Just as he tempted Jesus in the wilderness, trying to get Him to skip the suffering that would precede the Resurrection, so Satan will try to make us impatiently jump the gun. Every one of those wilderness temptations was crafted to get Jesus to take matters into His own hands, to shortcut God's timing.

When Satan tempted the hungry Jesus to turn stones into bread, he was basically saying, "You don't have to wait for God. You're hungry now. You're able to do this on your own. Do it now." Jesus's reply was priceless. If I might paraphrase: "Life is not about getting what I want now. It's about being in unbroken fellowship with the Father—waiting on His perfect timing and provision."

Am I reading too much into it? I don't think so. Not when we consider Jesus's statement later on: "I am the bread that gives life. He who comes to me will never be hungry. He who believes in me will never be thirsty" (John 6:35 ICB). No matter how much we think that our own dreams will satisfy the hunger of our souls, the only thing that can truly accomplish that is walking in fellowship with God—in His timing and according to His plan.

When Jesus shut the devil down in the first round, Satan went for a second. He took Jesus to a high mountain and offered Him all the authority to rule the kingdoms of this world if He would bow down and worship him. Jesus's answer is classic: "Get behind Me, Satan! For it is written, 'You shall worship the LORD your God, and Him only you shall serve'" (Luke 4:8).

The devil was offering Jesus something that was already His. Jesus later told His disciples: "All authority has been given to Me in heaven and on earth" (Matthew 28:18). Satan urged Jesus to frustrate God's plan and His perfect timing by taking authority and glory right then and there—before the Cross. Jesus knew that God's plan was to give all authority to the Son later—after the Cross. The devil does the same thing with us. He tempts us to achieve our dreams now—before the cross of purification and perfection. It's a timing thing.

One might think the devil would give up after two tries, but he launched a third attack. He even had the audacity to tempt Jesus with the Word of God (see Matthew 4:6). I'll paraphrase it to show the insolence a little more clearly: "If you are God's Son, throw Yourself down off this temple. God won't let any harm come to You if you are really His Son. That's what the Bible says!" Jesus didn't jump—not off the temple and not at the bait. Instead, He responded with the Word in a way that makes me think He probably gave the devil a pretty stern look as well: "It has been said, 'You shall not tempt the LORD your God'" (Luke 4:12).

It's my personal opinion on this verse, but I don't think Jesus was talking about the Father in His statement. I think Jesus was looking straight at Satan and saying, "Back off, Bubba! I'm Lord. You know it and I know it, so let's quit fooling around here." Satan was trying to get Jesus to play His hand before the Father's timing, but Jesus was not moved from His position of trusting in God's perfect timing for the revelation of His position as Savior.

Now let's overlay these same facts and principles onto Joseph's story. Potiphar needed someone to work for him. Did he need someone to work for him a month before Joseph arrived on the scene? Two months? Why was Potiphar even looking for someone right then to help him with his affairs? From the pit to the Midianite slave train to the marketplace where Joseph encountered Potiphar, God orchestrated the details of heaven's dream for Joseph's life. His dream was never at risk of belonging to someone else. Heaven's dreams for our lives are not negotiable. They only seem tenuous when we don't understand God's perfect timing and sovereignty.

So our dreams are not for sale. My dream is my dream, and no one can change that. God has promised a specific and unique plan for each one of us (see Jeremiah 29:11). The God who spans the universe with His hand will move heaven and earth to accomplish His plan. I know this to be true. I want to see that plan unfold, and I want it to unfold in God's timing, not mine.

Joseph's dreams were not for sale either. He would see his dreams come true, but before that could take place, there would have to be another change, a further understanding. His gratification would be delayed a while longer because God's perfect timing had not yet fully come. The same is true for us.

the *prison*

A few years back I went fishing with a group of friends. The trip had been planned with great anticipation. We weren't just going to sit on the side of a lake and fish for bass. No, we were after marlin. We were going out on the ocean in my boat to run with the "big boys." I figured we'd be out there for a while, so we stocked the boat with bait, lunch, drinks, and snacks. All the gear was ready. The morning was picture perfect. We got up early and headed out onto the vast expanse of water.

I rigged a pole and threw my line into the water to wet it. With the cool ocean breeze in my face, the smell of salt water in my nostrils, and the warmth of the sun rising over the horizon, my soul enjoyed one of those unplanned worship moments. You know the kind—when your heart is just so grateful for all that God has done.

We hadn't been out ten minutes when suddenly I heard what every fisherman lives for—the whir of my reel spinning. I couldn't believe it. I hadn't even reached my destination when this fish took my line out almost one hundred yards. *I got the big one!* I thought.

I stopped the boat. Everyone's eyes were on me. I pulled up my fishing rod and began to bring the fish in, when it suddenly shot up out of the water. It was a marlin and had to be at least eight feet long. The fish was white and blue with a long nose and a big spike on his back. This fish jumped in and out of the waves so rapidly and with such grace that he looked as though he were dancing. It was magnificent. My heart was thumping, and I couldn't stop thinking, *I've got the fish we're all out here for, and we're only ten minutes into our day!*

I worked to bring that amazing creature in, but it put up a tremendous fight. Soon every muscle in my body ached; my vision was blurred from the sweat dripping into my eyes. I kept thinking about Ernest Hemingway and *The Old Man and the Sea*. I was him! I was Santiago, and I had the fish of a lifetime. I heard myself vowing, much like the old man, "Fish, I'll stay with you until I am dead."

On the journey toward making our dreams reality, we rarely enjoy smooth sailing.

After what seemed like forever, I got the fish to within ten feet of the boat. My buddy had a gaff in his hand ready to help me bring the marlin on board. Just about the time I was mentally stuffing him and putting him above my mantel, the fish looked my direction. My gaze locked with one big, black eye. In an instant burned in my memory forever, that fish twisted his head from left to right, snapped the line, and took off. I was left only with the sweat, sore muscles, and the tantalizing memory of what might have been.

I was stunned. *Did this just happen? One of the biggest fish I'll ever hope to catch in my lifetime was within my reach, and in one second, this entire event became just another fish story!*

How many of our dreams are just fish stories now? Did one get away that has left us stunned and immobilized?

Joseph was on his way to a similar experience. Although Joseph had been sold into slavery, God was prospering him in his captivity. It seemed for a time that he might be getting the catch of a lifetime in comparison with the pit, but then the "big one" vanished before his very eyes. He would discover, as we all do on the journey toward making our dreams reality, that we rarely enjoy smooth sailing. On the contrary, as we saw in the previous chapter, often we no sooner get out of the pit than Satan launches his next ploy against us—to discourage us in the marketplace of our dreams. Then, once we realize that heaven's dreams for us are not up for grabs, Satan launches his third attack—to throw our dreams behind bars. We can see this final scene of hell's nightmare play out in Joseph's life in Genesis 39 and 40.

The Lesson of the Bars

From the pit into the hands of the Midianites and then on to the household of Potiphar, Joseph's lot improved dramatically. Potiphar happened to be an influential man of high rank in Pharaoh's administration who soon recognized that God had His hand on Joseph. Joseph earned a privileged position in Potiphar's service:

> *The LORD was with Joseph and blessed him greatly as he served in the home of his Egyptian master. Potiphar noticed this and realized that the LORD was with Joseph, giving him success in everything he did. So Joseph naturally became quite a favorite with him. Potiphar soon put Joseph in charge of his entire household and entrusted him with all his business dealings. From the day Joseph was put in charge, the LORD began to bless Potiphar for Joseph's sake. All his household affairs began to run smoothly, and his crops and livestock flourished. So Potiphar gave Joseph complete administrative responsibility over everything he owned. With Joseph there, he didn't have a worry in the world, except to decide what he wanted to eat!*

Now Joseph was a very handsome and well-built young man. (Genesis 39:2–6 NLT)

Sure, the pit had been unpleasant, and being sold was degrading, but Joseph must have been thinking that finally there was a little light at the end of the tunnel. Although being a slave would never compare with his position as a free, favored son of a wealthy Israelite, it sure beat being dead or being sold to a cruel taskmaster of lower means. At least in Potiphar's household there was hope that God might somehow restore the dream that would bring provision to share, power to save, and a position to shine. Joseph was given a position second to none other than Potiphar himself. He was in charge of everything—just like in his dream. Nothing happened in Potiphar's house that didn't need Joseph's stamp of approval. He had complete control.

Or did he?

A Satanic Setup

Even with everything seeming to go Joseph's way, Satan was setting him up. The Enemy had a plan to disrupt Joseph's dream once again, and he enrolled Potiphar's wife to accomplish it. For good reason, the Bible makes a point of noting that Joseph was a handsome and well-built young man. Apparently, Potiphar's wife was a woman with wandering eyes and loose scruples. She had her eye on Joseph, and she was used to getting her way.

Genesis 39:7 tells us, "His master's wife cast longing eyes on Joseph, and she said, 'Lie with me.'"

This is what a guy might call the direct approach. It's not so apparent in the New King James Version, but the New International Version reads this way: "Come to bed with me!" That's why we call it the direct approach. This was not a woman saying, "Uh, could you counsel me for a few sessions? I'd like to talk just to you. You're the only one who can help me." This is, "I want you now! NOW! I need you now! NOW!"

I love Joseph's response: "Joseph refused. 'Look,' he told her, 'my master trusts me with everything in his entire household. No one here has more authority than I do! He has held back nothing from me except you, because you are his wife. How could I ever do such a wicked thing? It would be a great sin against God'" (Genesis 39:8–9 NLT).

Unfortunately for Joseph, Potiphar's wife didn't take no for an answer. She was tenacious and made advance after advance: "She kept putting pressure on him day after day, but he refused to sleep with her, and he kept out of her way as much as possible" (Genesis 39:10 NLT).

Joseph didn't listen to her or give in to her. He didn't try to snuggle up or play around with the idea. He didn't even want to be near her. He made every effort to avoid this woman. Every time she made an advance, every time she drew close, every time she used a new tactic, he made a conscious choice to go in the opposite direction. I'm so proud of Joseph because he demonstrated that it can be done, even with an assertive woman making daily advances for who knows how many years. Joseph was probably around seventeen years old when his brothers sold him into slavery (see Genesis 37:2) and thirty when he came to power in Egypt (see Genesis 41:46). We know that he spent two years in prison prior to coming to power (see Genesis 41:1). That would mean he probably lived in Potiphar's house for about eleven years, from the age of seventeen to twenty-eight. These would have been the years of his sexual prime.

I'm belaboring the point because I want to make clear the magnitude of Joseph's situation. Perhaps we could bring this into better perspective if we set the whole scenario in modern times. Joseph's circumstances would be the equivalent of a young man, eighteen to twenty-nine years old, staying with his boss and having his boss's wife hitting on him every day. It would be tough even for the morally strongest of men to resist such temptation.

Joseph certainly could have rationalized his need and hers. He could have done the mental gymnastics we often do when we're looking for a reason to give in to sin. It goes something like this: *Why is it that Potiphar never meets his wife's needs? He's always off doing business. Why is it that she has such a deep desire to be with me? Why is it, Lord, that You continue to play games with my dream? Why is it, Lord, that I'm in this house right now with all these desires, and she has the same desires? Lord, could this actually be You arranging this circumstance so I can be a friend to her in her time of need?*

You may think my imagination is a little too liberal. I'd love to agree, but this rationale isn't coming from my imagination. I've borrowed it from real-life reasoning I've actually heard some Christians use to justify their base and wicked behavior in circumstances similar to Joseph's. But even though Potiphar's wife tempted him day after day, Joseph didn't fall into Satan's trap.

The Injustice of Prison

Joseph emphatically and repeatedly refused to sleep with Potiphar's wife. He sent the message, No, no, no, no, *no!* It's not going to happen, so just back off. Don't do this to me. Your husband trusts me, and I am not going to blow that trust. You're his wife. I will not sin against God in this way. Quit asking me!

Joseph stood firm in his refusal, but Potiphar's wife was not easily dissuaded. Finally she forced the issue, and suddenly Joseph saw the hope of his dream's coming to pass twist its head, break the line, and leave him with just another fish story:

She came and grabbed him by his shirt, demanding, "Sleep with me!" Joseph tore himself away, but as he did, his shirt came off. She was left holding it as he ran from the house.

When she saw that she had his shirt and that he had fled, she began screaming. Soon all the men around the place came running. "My husband has brought this Hebrew slave here to insult us!" she sobbed. "He tried to rape me, but I screamed. When he heard my loud cries, he ran and left his shirt behind with me."

She kept the shirt with her, and when her husband came home that night, she told him her story. "That Hebrew slave you've had around here tried to make a fool of me," she said. "I was saved only by my screams. He ran out, leaving his shirt behind!"

After hearing his wife's story, Potiphar was furious! He took Joseph and threw him into the prison where the king's prisoners were held. (Genesis 39:12–20 NLT)

Talk about a curve ball. Joseph had started to see a way his dream might be realized. He had made it through the pit and the marketplace. He had found favor in Potiphar's eyes. But then, through no fault of his own, he found himself behind bars. We can just picture him sitting in prison when a fellow inmate says, "Hey, buddy, what are you in for?"

"What am I in for? You wouldn't believe what happened. I was living right—faithfully, honestly, and sincerely—when the bottom fell out, and it's all because of some dream. I dreamed that one day I would be in a position of power. It wasn't even my dream—it was from God. But when I told my brothers about it, they got mad and threw me in a pit. Fortunately I was sold to Potiphar, and it looked like God might use that platform to finally make my dream come true. But then I was wrongfully accused and thrown behind bars."

Did Joseph's thoughts scream heavenward with the questions that come in times of trial? *Is this what You do to dreams? Is this what I can expect in a life where You are Lord? Well, I wish I'd never had that wretched dream in the first place. I can't believe how this has worked out. I mean, You gave me this dream, You planted this hope—but then You yanked the rug right out from under me. Is this some kind of cosmic game? Thank You very much, but I don't want to play anymore!*

Was Joseph sitting in his cell of circumstance chewing sour grapes? This had to be getting on his nerves. After all, he hadn't done anything wrong. In fact, he'd done everything right. He'd refused to sleep with Potiphar's wife, and for that he'd been thrown in jail. If he had slept with her, maybe he'd still be enjoying his privileged position and a relationship on the side.

We've all heard horror stories of honest businessmen who got bamboozled by their not-so-honest partners. We don't have to think too far back to remember how many hard-working, moral people got royally ripped off in the scandals of Enron and other corporate financial misconduct. How many times have we heard of or been part of a story in which a kindness was shown to someone who took advantage of the benevolence? Or what about a marriage in which one partner faithfully loves the other, who is having extramarital affairs?

One might wonder whether pursuing a dream is worthwhile. And that's exactly where Satan wants to take us and leave us—behind the bars of discouragement, giving up. Satan wants to derail our dreams and disrupt our hopes. He wants to throw us into a dungeon of disbelief, where he can kill our dreams.

The Justice of Prison

Perhaps the bars of our prison are less tangible or clear-cut. Maybe they're thoughts like, *This is never going to happen.* Or, *Forget the whole dream thing. Will you please not talk about dreams anymore? If you bring dreams up one more time, I don't think I can handle it. I've had it with the whole dream thing, OK? It's not going to happen. Just leave it that way.*

Or perhaps our bars sound like this: *Don't even ask me to pray for my family again, OK? They're just not turning to Christ. Do you have any idea how rebellious my kids are? Do you know what my parents said to me last week? Prayer isn't going to change anything.* Or this: *Don't even ask me to reinvest in this business. It's failing. I may have thought it would be successful, and I may have thought You called me to it, but it's just not happening, and I'm not going to keep trying.*

Often we don't recognize these as prison bars because we see them as situations for which we're partly responsible.

Our church received a call a while back from a man at a correctional institution. This is not unusual; from time to time we provide teaching tapes for prison libraries. Some of you in literal prisons may be thinking, *Bob, I did this to myself. I'm responsible for putting myself behind prison bars through the choices I made, so I can't even hope to realize heaven's dream after being such a poor manager of that dream.*

That thinking isn't so different from what those of us behind figurative bars often believe: that our dreams haven't—and never will—come true because we've failed.

May I say to those who are in prison—and to those who feel like you're in prison because of the agonizing consequences of poor choices—you are still in the running for a God-given dream.

Yes, many times we do put ourselves behind bars by our own actions.

> May I say to those who are in prison—and to those who feel like you're in prison because of the agonizing consequences of poor choices— you are still in the running for a God-given dream.

We fall for Satan's lie that if we don't do something to make things happen, they won't happen. We don't trust God for the future. In our lack of faith, we erect defensive walls around our hearts and think, *It's just not going to happen for me.* We decide that the provision we've been given will never be sufficient to share. We determine that our power will never be adequate to save. We conclude that the position we've been given never will provide us with the opportunity to shine. We believe all of this because God has not fulfilled our expectations. And we jump the gun on God's timing, only to find ourselves trapped in prison.

Have we bought the Enemy's lie that our dreams will never come to pass? If we take his bait, the devil will throw us behind bars before we know what has happened. We must not let him. If we do, we won't learn the next lesson necessary to defeat the Enemy and realize our dreams.

Our Faithful Endurance

God does not leave us alone behind bars. On the contrary, when we're in the prison of discouragement, He's getting ready to teach us one of the most important lessons yet—the value of perseverance. That's the point of prison.

When is the last day of the trial before we see our dreams realized? We don't know. Because we've been waiting so long—six months or maybe six years—we're sure there must still be a long wait ahead. But in reality, we might be right on the brink of seeing our dreams fulfilled.

Joseph's dream would come to pass before long, but for a time he remained behind bars. The bars were obstacles, but a pattern that seemed to be developing helped him hold on to the hope of his dream. Yet again, in Joseph's unfortunate set of circumstances, the Lord's hand was upon him:

> *After hearing his wife's story, Potiphar was furious! He took Joseph and threw him into the prison where the king's prisoners were held. But the LORD was with Joseph there, too, and he granted Joseph favor with the chief jailer. Before long, the jailer put Joseph in charge of all the other prisoners and over everything that happened in the prison. The chief jailer had no more worries after that, because Joseph took care of every-*

thing. The LORD was with him, making everything run smoothly and successfully. (Genesis 39:19–23 NLT)

God put Joseph in a privileged position even within the confines of his circumstances. This recurring display of God's favor gave Joseph the ability to keep hoping for the fulfillment of his dream even when prison bars stood in the way.

Our own quests to see heaven's dreams made real in our lives are like this. Though we may have the dreams in sight, that doesn't mean there aren't obstacles to overcome. Jesus said, "I have told you all this so that you may have peace in me. Here on earth you will have many trials and sorrows. But take heart, because I have overcome the world" (John 16:33 NLT). Jesus overcame the world, but we are still in the world and thus will face many hurdles, trials, and barriers on our quests to fulfill God's dreams for our lives. If we're going to succeed, we must persevere in spite of difficulties.

Even when we get thrown a curve ball, God is still with us and still in control. But we need faith to believe that. The Bible defines faith this way: "Faith means being sure of the things we hope for. And faith means knowing that something is real even if we do not see it" (Hebrews 11:1 ICB). One of my colleagues gives a working definition of faith that I like: "Faith is believing God is good when circumstances aren't."

Faith is critical in our pursuit of heaven's dreams for this reason: "Without faith it is impossible to please Him [God], for he who comes to God must believe that He is, and that He is a rewarder of those who diligently seek Him" (Hebrews 11:6).

If our dreams are God's dreams, and since it's God's power that fulfills those dreams, then we need to work with God rather than working against Him. How do we do this? The Bible tells us that "'God is against the proud, but he gives grace to the humble'" (James 4:6 ICB).

A prideful person is one who is self-reliant, determined to fulfill his or her own dream in his or her own strength. A humble person is one who wants God's dream only and knows that the fulfillment of His dream will require His strength. Faith clearly understands that the dreams belong to God and that we desperately need God's grace to accomplish them. Only when we operate in conjunction with God through faith can we ever be assured of overcoming every obstacle, because only God is in absolute control, and so many things are beyond our own control.

It has been well said that there are two things that should never anger us—those things we can change and those things we can't. What could I do about the fish that got away? I can bait my line a little bit better and make sure I'm using stronger fiber for my fishing line.

What could Joseph do about being thrown into prison? The very thing he did do: he continued to have faith in his God-given dream despite the obstacles that were in his way. How do I know that? Let's go back to the story:

> It came to pass after these things that the butler and the baker of the king of Egypt offended their lord, the king of Egypt. And Pharaoh was angry with his two officers, the chief butler and the chief baker. So he put them in custody in the house of the captain of the guard, in the prison, the place where Joseph was confined. And the captain of the guard charged Joseph with them, and he served them; so they were in custody for a while.
>
> Then the butler and the baker of the king of Egypt, who were confined in the prison, had a dream, both of them, each man's dream in one night and each man's dream with its own interpretation. And Joseph came in to them in the morning and looked at them, and saw that they were sad. So he asked Pharaoh's officers who were with him in the custody of his lord's house, saying, "Why do you look so sad today?"

And they said to him, "We each have had a dream, and there is no interpreter of it."

So Joseph said to them, "Do not interpretations belong to God? Tell them to me, please." (Genesis 40:1–8)

Did you catch it? This is how we can tell that Joseph still had faith. When Joseph asked why they were sad, the butler and baker replied, "We had a dream." Notice how Joseph did not respond. He did not say, "Oh, please, stop with the dream thing. Do you have any idea why I'm in prison in the first place? Do you know that I'm here because of a dream? Don't even talk to me about dreams!" He didn't say that.

Similarly, if we've had some bad relationships and someone says excitedly, "I'm getting married," how we respond will reveal a great deal about our faith. Will we say, "Oh, please, don't talk to me about marriage—all men are idiots," or, "all women are crazy."

What if a buddy says, "I just signed papers to start a company. I'm looking forward to working with my new partner." Do we answer with sarcasm because we've failed in business not just once but twice? Do we cynically discourage this friend with comments like, "You're crazy to trust a partner. Don't you know that people are only out for number one? Everyone is a liar and a cheat when it comes to money."

Responses like these are sure signs of failing faith. But Joseph enthusiastically answered the butler and the baker in a way that demonstrated his faith: "You had a dream? Really? Did you know that God is the interpreter of dreams? If you tell them to me, I can ask Him for the interpretation because I have a relationship with God that is still vibrant and vital, even when my own dreams seem unattainable."

Did God give Joseph the interpretation? Yes He did, because He rewards those who diligently seek Him through faith. Let's look at what happened:

The chief butler told his dream to Joseph, and said to him, "Behold, in my dream a vine was before me, and in the vine were three branches; it was as though it budded, its blossoms shot forth, and its clusters brought forth ripe grapes. Then Pharaoh's cup was in my hand; and I took the grapes and pressed them into Pharaoh's cup, and placed the cup in Pharaoh's hand." And Joseph said to him, "This is the interpretation of it: The three branches are three days. Now within three days Pharaoh will lift up your head and restore you to your place, and you will put Pharaoh's cup in his hand according to the former manner, when you were his butler. But remember me when it is well with you, and please show kindness to me; make mention of me to Pharaoh, and get me out of this house. For indeed I was stolen away from the land of the Hebrews; and also I have done nothing here that they should put me into the dungeon." (Genesis 40:9–15)

Great dream! The baker listened to the favorable interpretation of the butler's dream and was encouraged to share his own dream:

When the chief baker saw that the interpretation was good, he said to Joseph, "I also was in my dream, and there were three white baskets on my head. In the uppermost basket were all kinds of baked goods for Pharaoh, and the birds ate them out of the basket on my head."

So Joseph answered and said, "This is the interpretation of it: The three baskets are three days. Within three days Pharaoh will lift off your head from you and hang you on a tree; and the birds will eat your flesh from you." (Genesis 40:16–19)

The baker had to be thinking, *Uh, could I have a different interpretation? Do you think you could go back and pray again to see if you get something different?* And Joseph must have been tempted to alter the interpretation of the baker's dream. I mean, who wants to be the bearer of this kind of news?

But Joseph's faith was so intact that he resisted that temptation to change what God said. Joseph had learned well the lessons of the pit, the marketplace, and the prison, that in God's sovereignty there is no need to try to manipulate circumstances. The fate of the baker was in God's hands, not Joseph's. Joseph knew that, so he continued to do what he could and accepted the things he couldn't change as being in the providence of God—even in prison.

No matter where we are, God will lead us step by step. If we follow faithfully, we'll be right on track. Joseph's imprisonment was not a mistake. It was part of God's plan.

The Products of Perseverance

Whatever our bars of opposition may be, we need to remember that they're also our opportunities to persevere and achieve our dreams. Think about the countless men and women in our world who have realized their dreams. One trait they all possessed is perseverance.

Often ridiculed, Edison tried over ten thousand different experiments before he finally successfully developed the first incandescent light bulb on October 21, 1879.[1]

Henry Ford suffered two unsuccessful attempts to build his dream with the Detroit Automobile Company and the Henry Ford Company before succeeding.[2]

Abraham Lincoln lost more than half a dozen elections before he became the sixteenth president of the United States.[3]

The Wright brothers failed 147 times before they built an airplane that could fly.[4]

What if Edison had quit one try before he made it? What if the Wright brothers had decided they were tired of crashing just one flight before they succeeded? What if Lincoln had let his losses determine his legacy? Perseverance is what makes a leader, a visionary, and a success of anyone who goes after a dream.

God uses prison bars to build our strength and character. He tells us that when we look at these obstacles through the eyes of faith, they can actually be cause for joy: "Dear brothers and sisters, whenever trouble comes your way, let it be an opportunity for joy. For when your faith is tested, your endurance has a chance to grow. So let it grow, for when your endurance is fully developed, you will be strong in character and ready for anything" (James 1:2–4 NLT).

That's an amazing statement. Wouldn't you love to be ready for anything this life throws at you? I would. I'd love to wake up each morning and know that whatever happens, I'm ready for it. The Bible says that if we allow God to develop perseverance in our lives through times of trial, we'll be able to handle the hard times.

A secondary benefit of perseverance is one that's never known by people who quit. As a parent I've noticed that my kids are not very thankful for things that are just handed to them. But if I make them work for what they receive, they value the prize and are likely to take better care of it. Similarly, when our heavenly Father teaches us perseverance through trials and tribulation, our realization of heaven's dreams in our lives is that much sweeter.

The pit purifies our understanding that our dreams are really God's dreams. The marketplace helps us see that God is sovereign and that heaven's dreams for our lives are nonnegotiable. But the prison gives us the final ingredient necessary to attain our dreams: perseverance. Without the ability to stay the course, we'll stop before we get to walk in the reality of our dreams—maybe just short of the goal. It's this perseverance, this tenacity, this never-say-die attitude that keeps us going until we attain heaven's dreams.

Author Irving Stone has spent a lifetime studying greatness, writing novelized biographies of such men as Michelangelo, Vincent van Gogh, Sigmund Freud, and Charles Darwin. Stone was once asked if he had found a thread that runs through the lives of all these exceptional people.

He said, "I write about people who sometime in their life . . . have a vision or dream of something that should be accomplished . . . and they go to work. They are beaten over the head, knocked down, vilified, and for years they get nowhere. But every time they're knocked down, they stand up. You cannot destroy these people. And at the end of their lives they've accomplished some modest part of what they set out to do."[5]

Listen to just a few such stories of great perseverance:

Bette Nesmith had a good secretarial job in a Dallas bank when she ran across a problem that interested her. Wasn't there a better way to correct the errors she made on her electric typewriter? Bette had some art experience, and she knew that artists who worked in oils just painted over their errors. Maybe that would work for her too. So she concocted a fluid to paint over her typing errors. Before long, all the secretaries in her building were using what she then called "MistakeOut." She attempted to sell the product idea to marketing agencies and various companies (including IBM), but they turned her down. However, secretaries continued to like her product, so Bette Nesmith's kitchen became her first manufacturing facility, and she started selling it on her own. When Bette Nesmith sold the enterprise, the tiny white bottles were earning $3.5 million annually on sales of $38 million. The buyer was Gillette Company, and the sale price was $47.5 million.[6]

One day George Müller began praying for five of his friends. After many months one of them came to the Lord. Ten years later two others were converted. It took 25 years before the fourth man was saved. Müller persevered in prayer until his death for the fifth friend, and throughout those 52 years he never gave up hoping that he would accept Christ! His faith was rewarded, for soon after Müller's funeral the last one was saved.[7]

Florence Chadwick was the first woman to swim the English Channel in both directions. On the Fourth of July in 1951, she attempted to swim from Catalina Island to the California coast. The challenge was not so much the distance. The challenge was the bone-chilling waters of the Pacific. To complicate matters, a dense fog lay over the entire area, making it impossible for her to see land. After about 15 hours in the water, and within a half mile of her goal, Chadwick gave up. Later she told a reporter, "Look, I'm not excusing myself. But if I could have seen land, I might have made it." Not long afterward she attempted the feat again. Once more a misty veil obscured the coastline, and she couldn't see the shore. But this time she made it because she kept reminding herself that land was there. With that confidence she bravely swam on and achieved her goal. In fact, she broke the men's record by 2 hours![8]

Consider these famous people who were slow starters but who didn't give up, according to the Chattanooga Resource Foundation:

- Winston Churchill seemed so dull as a youth that his father thought he might be incapable of earning a living in England.

- G. K. Chesterton, the English writer, could not read until he was eight. One of his teachers told him, "If we could open your head, we should not find any brain but only a lump of white fat."

- Thomas Edison's first teacher described him as "addled," and his father almost convinced him he was a "dunce."

- Albert Einstein's parents feared their child was dull, and he performed so badly in all high-school courses except mathematics that a teacher asked him to drop out.[9]

Most of us are familiar with New York Yankee Joe DiMaggio, a two-time American League Most Valuable Player, and one of the greatest baseball players ever. What some may not know is that he played with injuries through much of his career. Yet he was the American League's MVP twice.[10] He didn't achieve this by giving up. He did it by persevering.

Dreams That Never Die

How about you? Were you on track to fulfill your dreams when you encountered a detour, and now your dreams seem like they've all but died? Maybe you're like Joseph and were doing everything right.

What makes you quit? Is it the fish that got away, the seductive temptation, or the million other small and large obstacles Satan places in your path? If you're prone to quit, you're probably thinking about putting down this book right now. Go ahead. Walk away. No more dreaming, no more hoping, no more inspiration, no more aspiration, no hopes for greatness for you.

Is that really the alternative to persevering? Yes, unfortunately it is. That's why we find so many of our fellow travelers settling into run-of-the-mill lives devoid of dreams and on a slow road to nowhere. Hopeless, aimless, uninspired mediocrity is what awaits quitters.

But can I let you in on a little secret? Even if that's where you are now, you don't have to stay there. The truth is that dreams never die. Sometimes the dreamer inside us dies, but God can bring that dreamer back to life. That's what redemption is all about. God wants to restore your hope. He wasn't finished with Joseph even when he was in prison in Egypt, and He's definitely not finished with you.

If your dream has been derailed, decide right now that you won't stay off track. Persevere with me to the next stop on our journey and find out how God brings life back to the dreamer and restores the dream. Keep going—you're almost there.

Part Three

Our *Reality*

dreams *redeemed*

Recently I was working on a one-hundred-piece puzzle with my son. We had only five pieces left, but we just couldn't seem to make them fit, even though we were sure that every other piece had been properly placed. In the remaining section of the puzzle, all of the colors were so well blended that we really had to focus on the shape as well as the color, and even the shapes themselves were very similar. We were incredibly frustrated yet determined, almost frantic, to finish our project. Just when we felt that we were never going to figure it out, we finally hit the right combination. What jubilation we felt when the last piece fell into place. It was amazing how those last few pieces were some of the hardest ones to put in place.

We're now approaching the last few pieces of this dream puzzle. The truths conveyed in the next few chapters will be some of the hardest ones to put in place. As we look at how God redeems our dreams and makes them realities in our lives, we'll find that He actually designs life like a puzzle for a reason.

When I was a kid, my mom and dad gave me a bike for Christmas, but they didn't put it under the tree. My dad knew that a quest to find an elusive present could be almost more fun than the gift itself. To this day I remember the excitement that ran through my veins as I looked for that bike. I got more and more worked up with each new clue that led me closer to the prize.

Easter baskets were always hidden, too, in the Coy household. My siblings and I never came down the stairs to baskets just sitting there with our names on them. They were concealed because part of the joy was in finding them. And my mom and dad had as much fun watching us find what they'd hidden as we had finding it. Perhaps that's the point of this proverb: "It is the glory of God to conceal a matter; to search out a matter is the glory of kings" (Proverbs 25:2 NIV).

The Father Heart of God

God is a heavenly Father who is into hide-and-seek. He loves when we possess a spirit of adventure and look for something with all our hearts. He knows the discovery will be all the better for the quest. He even tells us that we can't expect to find Him unless we put our whole hearts into it: "You will seek me and find me when you seek me with all your heart" (Jeremiah 29:13 NIV).

When we think about those things in life for which we had to wait the longest, believe the hardest, and trust God the most, we'll realize that they also happen to be the things we now value and appreciate more than the things that came easily. God loves the hide-and-seek of life because it requires faith. Faith is what enables us to endure, believe, and trust in what we can't see. This is critical, because while in the process of waiting for what we can't see, we are being transformed into the likeness of God, whom we also can't see. In fact, we are hard-wired with the longing to find what is concealed because that desire is what brings us into relationship with an invisible God.

This insatiable desire for the hunt begins early. From pretending to be pirates looking for hidden treasure to the game of hide-and-seek where we look for a hidden person, as kids we were always looking for something. I think children instinctively understand that what they're looking for often isn't nearly as exciting or valuable as the expedition itself. That's why when we finally did uncover the hidden playmate, Easter eggs, or whatever else we pursued, we just started all over again. As adults we tend to forget this, and we become disillusioned when what we seek and find doesn't bring more permanent satisfaction.

What makes God's game of hide-and-seek unique is that the find is ongoing. Not only can we experience the thrill of the chase, but we don't have to suffer disappointment at our destination because our quest doesn't end there. In fact, it's in the discovery that the adventure truly begins.

> God loves the hide-and-seek of life because it requires faith. Faith is what enables us to endure, believe, and trust in what we can't see.

As we've progressed through this book, we've seen that God is kind, benevolent, gracious, merciful, and loving. We've noted that although we have an enemy who is out to destroy us, God is in control of everything, including the actions of our adversary. And now we see that God is a loving Father who wants us to have a little fun on our journeys. So He hides a few things. If we have a relationship with God and understand that He has our best interests in mind, we can enjoy the treasure hunt. But for those who are still in a place of indecision about God, this idea of God playing games with us might be a bit unnerving. Yet the only way to move forward in the quest to make heaven's dreams our realities is to trust Him and decide that we really want heaven's dreams with all they entail.

What exactly does it mean to trust God and accept His plans for our lives instead of our own? It means we relinquish all of our hopes, desires, and aspirations in this life. In return, however, we get His hopes, desires, and aspirations for us, not just in this life but in the next life as well. We exchange our limited means for the limitless resources of an infinite God. When we give up our lives for the lives God has planned for us, we get Jesus in the transaction. That's what the apostle Paul was talking about when he said, "I myself no longer live, but Christ lives in me. So I live my life in this earthly body by trusting in the Son of God, who loved me and gave himself for me" (Galatians 2:20 NLT).

That means that all God has called us to be and do is possible because He lives in us. Paul further affirmed this fact in his letter to the church in Philippi: "Keep on working to complete your salvation, and do it with fear and trembling. Yes, God is working in you to help you want to do what pleases him. Then he gives you the power to do it" (Philippians 2:12–13 ICB).

This point becomes crucial when we consider that the exchange also means we have to stop walking by sight and instead embrace a life of faith. We can see how the exchange plays out in this passage of Scripture:

> *As we know Jesus better, his divine power gives us everything we need for living a godly life. He has called us to receive his own glory and goodness! And by that same mighty power, he has given us all of his rich and wonderful promises. He has promised that you will escape the decadence all around you caused by evil desires and that you will share in his divine nature.*
>
> *So make every effort to apply the benefits of these promises to your life. Then your faith will produce a life of moral excellence. A life of moral excellence leads to knowing God better. Knowing God leads to self-control. Self-control leads to patient endurance, and patient endurance leads to godliness. Godliness leads to love for other Christians, and finally you will grow to have genuine love for everyone. The more*

you grow like this, the more you will become productive and useful in your knowledge of our Lord Jesus Christ. (2 Peter 1:3–8 NLT)

God's endless resources are not found in the temporal realm of the here and now. They are found in His Word, and they are accessed by faith. Only as we walk in faith can we possess His promises that bring us to the fulfillment of our dreams.

The Faithful Promises of God

The Bible is full of God's promises, but we receive those promises first by faith. God's promises are for those who have made a decision to accept heaven's dreams for their lives. That means that in the present, we might not see the fulfillment of those promises because they are ours by faith. Hebrews 11:1 says, "Faith is the substance of things hoped for, the evidence of things not seen." While we wait for the evidence of things we do not yet see, God works to bring forth heaven's dreams in our lives.

During this waiting time, God's dream is coming true. His dream is for us to be conformed to His image—to be holy as He is holy (see 1 Peter 1:16). This process is what the Bible calls sanctification (see 1 Corinthians 6:11; Ephesians 5:25–27; 2 Thessalonians 2:13–14). But if God were to give us our dreams immediately, when would that sanctification happen? Without the wait, God would never have the chance to develop in us the qualities that are characteristic of Him, like purity, perfection, perseverance, and the ability to wait patiently.

Our society has forgotten the value of waiting. We're used to getting everything in a matter of seconds. I'm guilty. I find myself upgrading my computer because I don't want to wait more than a few nanoseconds for it to calculate what would take me hours to figure out. And I'm spoiled. I can take my suit to the dry cleaners and get it back in one hour.

Naturally, we transfer this expectation of instant gratification to the promises of God. We want our dreams to come true, and we want them to come true now! We suffer from the overwhelming anxiety that time is wasting and the world is passing us by. Because we're so unaccustomed to waiting, when we don't see immediate results, we become leery of God's intentions. We wonder, *Why is He taking so long? When is He going to bring this about? I know God is providing daily in many ways, but I'm still waiting outside the Promised Land. I should have settled for my self-driven dream—at least I could have made it happen by now.*

That's when we need to be careful. It's at just such a point that we often make the big mistake of stepping outside of God's will.

It wouldn't be the first time God has had to deal with human impatience, but when we find ourselves wanting the goods now rather than later, we would do well to remember a story from the book of Numbers. I'd rather we learn this lesson from the Israelites than have to go through it ourselves:

> *The mixed multitude who were among them yielded to intense craving; so the children of Israel also wept again and said: "Who will give us meat to eat? We remember the fish which we ate freely in Egypt, the cucumbers, the melons, the leeks, the onions, and the garlic; but now our whole being is dried up; there is nothing at all except this manna before our eyes!" . . .*
>
> *Then Moses heard the people weeping throughout their families, everyone at the door of his tent; and the anger of the LORD was greatly aroused; Moses also was displeased. . . .*
>
> *Now a wind went out from the LORD, and it brought quail from the sea and left them fluttering near the camp, about a day's journey on this side and about a day's journey on the other side, all around the camp, and about two cubits above the surface of the ground. And the people stayed up all that day, all night, and all the next day, and gathered the quail (he who gathered least gathered ten homers); and they spread them out for themselves all around the camp. But while the meat*

*was still between their teeth, before it was chewed, the wrath of the
LORD was aroused against the people, and the LORD struck the people
with a very great plague. So he called the name of that place Kibroth
Hattaavah, because there they buried the people who had yielded to
craving. (Numbers 11:4–6, 10, 31–34)*

God had promised the people of Israel a land flowing with milk and
honey. In the interim He provided manna to feed and sustain them on
their journey to the Promised Land. But rather than being thankful for
and content with what God had given them, they looked back longingly
on their bondage and complained. This angered the Lord. What I want
to point out for our benefit is the frightening way in which He dealt
with their ingratitude. God gave them the quail, but while they were
pigging out on it, He sent a plague.

An additional insight on this story can be found in the book of
Psalms. In recounting the story of the Israelites' pilgrimage from Egypt
to the Promised Land, the psalmist gave this revealing side note: "They
soon forgot His works; they did not wait for His counsel, but lusted ex-
ceedingly in the wilderness, and tested God in the desert. And He gave
them their request, but sent leanness into their soul" (Psalm 106:13–15).

God gave them what they wanted but sent leanness to their souls.
How sad. The Bible says, "It is worth nothing for a person to have the
whole world, if he loses his soul. A person could never pay enough to
buy back his soul" (Mark 8:36–37 ICB).

Maybe that's where you find yourself right now. You wanted the fulfillment of your dream so badly that you were willing to do almost anything to get it. And right now you're reading this book with a lean soul.
Maybe it's one of the reasons you picked up this book in the first place.
You knew something was missing from your life. Maybe you even got
the thing you thought would make you happy, only to find that it wasn't
all you had imagined it would be.

If you're in this dilemma, God can restore your soul. But the ball is in your court. One of the things you'll have to do is decide right now that you will trust God with your life. Then you'll have to wait for His best rather than settling for whatever dream you're holding on to or have been chasing on your own for so long. You must make that leap of faith to let go of what you can see and hold on to what you can't see until God has perfected His plan in your life.

How long will God's plan take? That's up to God, but the degree to which we let go of what we've been pursuing is the degree to which God can work in our lives to bring about heaven's dream. No surrender—no track. Half surrender—half-track. Total surrender—fast track.

If we're still hung up on the wait, perhaps it will help to consider things from God's vantage point. If His dream is that we become more and more like Him, think about how long He's been waiting for us.

My wife and I waited eleven years for our first child. From the first doctor's visit, the prognosis was not good. Having kids seemed for us an impossible dream. We felt as though we were in a deep, dark, empty pit. With each passing year, we experienced the anxiety and disappointment of watching our friends start families. It became painful to receive yet another birth announcement when our dream seemed so unattainable. With each baby dedication I performed monthly, I had to hope against hope that one day I would be dedicating my own son or daughter. It certainly seemed that my dream was being lived by everyone else in the congregation—even in the world—and that it would never happen in my own life.

> The longer we wait, the more complete we'll become because maturity is wrought in the process of waiting.

After two surgeries we still waited. We could see the possibility of having a child increasing ever so slightly, but always through the prison bars of knowing that neither my wife nor I were getting any younger. Each month brought only more heartbreaking barrenness. I can't even count the number of times I had to console my wife on Mother's Day when a well-meaning person would make some careless comment that left her devastated. She even stopped going to church on that holiday until after we had our first child.

Yet in spite of all the pain and the years of not knowing whether our dream would ever be realized, Diane and I agree that we're better parents today because of our long season of waiting. In the purification of the pit, in the perfection of the marketplace, and in the perseverance of the prison, we were made more and more into the image of our heavenly Father. Our children, Christian and Caitlyn, will be the blessed recipients of more grace, more mercy, more wisdom, more patience, more gentleness, more kindness, and even more godly discipline because of our wait.

If our dreams are fulfilled prematurely, we might come out halfbaked. The longer we wait, the more complete we'll become because maturity is wrought in the process of waiting. What's more important—God's dream coming true in our lives so we look more like Him, or achieving our own self-driven dreams that will be quickly eclipsed by the next self-driven dream? I hope through the final chapters of this book, we all will come to understand how inferior our own dreams are in comparison with heaven's dreams for us.

God's Timing

Do you honestly want to be a half-baked Christian, or do you want to wait until God says, "Well done"? Forgive me if my play on words is not very funny in light of your situation, but I prefer to lighten the impact of this message with a little humor.

I realize this is a tough concept, but there is a logical reason for our wait. That's why the prison lesson of endurance is necessary. Everything in God's plan has to do with proper timing. The Bible talks about the right time, or due time (see Daniel 12:7; Romans 5:6, 1 Peter 5:6). If we examine the life of Christ, we'll see that He kept to an immutable timetable. Scripture records that Jesus was born in the fullness of time (see Galatians 4:4), and throughout His earthly ministry, until the time came for Him to lay down His life (see Mark 14:41), the Bible indicates that it had not yet been His time to die (see John 7:8, 30; 8:20).

Jesus knew that every minute of every day was accounted for in His Father's plan, and He painstakingly kept on schedule. In the short three-and-a-half years of Jesus's ministry, He accomplished more than seemed humanly possible because He stayed in step with the Father. This ability so astounded the apostle John that he wrote, "Jesus did many other things as well. If every one of them were written down, I suppose that even the whole world would not have room for the books that would be written" (John 21:25 NIV).

The Bible tells us that God has ordained the number of our days (see Job 14:5); that He collects our tears in a bottle (see Psalm 56:8); and that He knows the number of hairs on our heads (see Matthew 10:30). God has thought through everything according to His omniscience and is orchestrating His plans for our lives according to His omnipotence.

God could have sent quail to the Israelites sooner or under different conditions. He has the power to do such things. He's doing something all the time. Just because we can't see it, let's not make the dangerous assumption that things aren't happening. Check the Bible sometime for all the phrases like "Then suddenly God," or "And then God," or "In the fullness of time, God . . ." Major undertakings are going on behind the scenes, in the spiritual realm. Jesus alluded to this when He said, "My Father never stops working. And so I work, too" (John 5:17 ICB).

God sovereignly and lovingly orchestrates all of time and eternity. He is coordinating every detail of His plan for us so that it interacts perfectly with every detail of the plans for other people, weaving them together like a holy tapestry.

All of the orchestration and detail centers on God's primary goal—to make us more like Him. He's looking for holiness in our lives. God says, "Be holy; for I am holy" (Leviticus 11:44). The word for *holy* in Greek (*hagios*) indicates a sanctification or consecration—a godlikeness. God wants us to be set apart for Him alone. Jesus also said, "You shall be perfect, just as your Father in heaven is perfect" (Matthew 5:48). The word *perfect* in Greek (*téleios*) signifies a state of being complete, mature, or fully grown in moral character. Together these verses reveal that God's dream is to have us all to Himself, as complete and mature as He is.

As a parent I can relate. There are things I love about my kids' ages, but I find it humorous that from time to time I catch myself telling my kids to stop acting like children. The truth is, however, they act like kids because they *are* kids. And though I love them dearly at any age, I'm looking forward to their growing up. I'm waiting for them to stop some of their childish behavior because there are many things we can't do together yet. I want to give them the keys to the car. I want to share deeper spiritual truths with them. I want to watch them with their kids. I can't do any of these things right now because they're not yet fully mature. I have to wait.

God is waiting too. He's waiting for us to grow up. He has big dreams for us. He wants to give us the keys to the kingdom. He wants to share deeper spiritual truths with us. He wants to watch us disciple baby believers. He has so many hidden treasures that are just begging to be discovered, but He's stuck waiting for us to mature enough to receive them. When will we grow up enough to remember what we knew as children—that life is about the journey toward discovery, not the prize itself? The real question is not how long we have to wait for God to fulfill our dreams, but how long does He have to wait for us to be ready?

Our Readiness

Behind bars Joseph was being made ready. He underwent an endurance test, and his faith was still vibrant enough that he could interpret the dreams of the butler and the baker. But could it stay healthy for two more years? It would have to, because that's how much longer Joseph would be stuck in prison.

That's right. Even after Joseph told the butler his dream was about to come true, that he would be restored to his position once he was delivered from prison, the butler forgot Joseph (see Genesis 40:23).

But God didn't forget.

God could have given Pharaoh his dream two years earlier to trigger the butler's memory of Joseph, but He didn't. The perceived delay of our dreams doesn't indicate God's inability; it has to do with our growth and who we are in Christ at that point.

Have you been praying for that special someone for a while now? Is there something God is still trying to do in you? If you're in a relationship and you've been praying for that relationship to improve, is there something God wants to work in your lives rather than sprinkling magic dust over your heads and making you a happy couple? Is there something in the Word of God concerning relationships that you must apply in order to reap the benefit of God's way of doing things?

By divine design, two years after Joseph interpreted the butler's and the baker's dreams, Pharaoh also had a dream (see Genesis 41:1–4). He saw seven fat cows and seven gaunt cows, and the gaunt cows ate the fat ones. His dream puzzled him, so he called for his mediums and soothsayers, but none of them could interpret the dream. Our modern-day equivalent of calling in soothsayers would be going to a psychic or astrologer. We can rest assured that when all the psychics in town can't answer our questions in life, God has a way of giving specific revelation. At last the butler remembered Joseph: "Hey, Pharaoh, I remember this guy in prison who interprets dreams. He told me I'd be restored to my position, and it happened just like he said."

So Joseph was brought from prison to interpret Pharaoh's dream. Note how Joseph deflected glory away from himself and to God in this declaration to Pharaoh: "I am not able to explain the meaning of dreams. God will do this for the king" (Genesis 41:16 ICB).

This amazing statement of faith demonstrates the fruit borne of Joseph's testing. Through the pit, the marketplace, the prison, and then two more years of waiting, trusting, and praying, Joseph had plenty of time to think things through. And in his season of waiting, he realized that he was not the dreamer.

Let that astounding truth sink in. We are not the dreamers. God is the dreamer. His dream fulfilled through us brings provision to share with others. That's why Christians should be the most generous of people—because God is so generous. It's also God's dream to use us to save others. We should all be evangelizing others because Christ died to save the world. And it is God's dream that whatever position we're in, we use it to shine. We should be lights to the world around us because Christ is the light of the world.

> God is the dreamer, and any fulfillment will be God living His dream through us by faith in Christ.

God is the dreamer, and any fulfillment will be God living His dream through us by faith in Christ. Scripture says it this way: "We are Christ's ambassadors, and God is using us to speak to you. We urge you, as though Christ himself were here pleading with you, 'Be reconciled to God!'" (2 Corinthians 5:20 NLT).

Earlier in that epistle, Paul wrote, "This precious treasure—this light and power that now shine within us—is held in perishable containers, that is, in our weak bodies. So everyone can see that our glorious power is from God and is not our own" (2 Corinthians 4:7 NLT).

God is the dreamer. We are the vessels, the instruments of fulfillment of His dream for mankind.

Hope or Hype

The difference between God-given dreams and self-driven dreams is the difference between hope and hype. We can chase fantasies all our lives, constructing a dream like a house of cards—the foundation built on all the propaganda of the Enemy, whom the Bible tells us is the father of lies (see John 8:44). But not only will our self-driven dreams fail because they're just facades, they'll also keep us so busy that we never discover our God-given dreams—which are better than any we could have imagined ourselves.

My own story bears this out dramatically. I spent years believing I could attain success and happiness without Christ. I even became somewhat successful by the world's standard—great job, nice car, luxurious apartment, the company of all the women I could possibly want, and no lack of buddies with whom to party. I even had times of pleasure, but as God's Word warns (see Hebrews 11:24–26), they were short-lived.

The most amazing discovery I made during that season of my life was that none of those trappings ever brought the peace, contentment, or significance for which my soul longed. As I look back now, I realize that my self-driven dream could never have delivered the joy, peace, and purpose I hoped it would. And that dream's failure prepared me to receive heaven's dream.

Never in my wildest imagination would I have thought I'd be living the dream I'm living today. I didn't see it, didn't plan it, and didn't even wish for it because I didn't have the capacity in my own intellect to know why I was created. My life is a dream beyond my ability to dream, but it's not amazing simply because of what it is. It's amazing because of how it puts me in the position for which I was designed.

What is our ultimate goal in life as human beings? Why do we strive with all that is in us to be rich and famous? Why do we seek relationship after relationship? What is it we're looking for? Is it not to find that one thing that brings ultimate joy, satisfaction, and a sense of purpose? Well, if we've been created by God with a specific plan in mind, then doesn't it stand to reason that the only way we'll ever be completely happy, satisfied, or content is to fulfill that purpose?

The apostle Paul was a man who was so in tune with the purpose for which God created him that what happened to him in this life had little or no influence over him. His joy, peace, and sense of significance did not depend on circumstances but rather came through his relationship with God. After years in service to Christ, at times living comfortably and at times living in the dungeons of Rome, he wrote,

I have learned to be satisfied with the things I have and with everything that happens. I know how to live when I am poor. And I know how to live when I have plenty. I have learned the secret of being happy at any time in everything that happens. I have learned to be happy when I have enough to eat and when I do not have enough to eat. I have learned to be happy when I have all that I need and when I do not have the things I need. I can do all things through Christ because he gives me strength. (Philippians 4:11–13 ICB)

Earlier in that letter, as Paul looked back at all the prestige, power, and accomplishments of his life before Christ, he explained,

At one time all these things were important to me. But now I think those things are worth nothing because of Christ. Not only those things, but I think that all things are worth nothing compared with the greatness of knowing Christ Jesus my Lord. Because of Christ, I have lost all those things. And now I know that all those things are worthless trash. This allows me to have Christ and to belong to him. Now that I belong to Christ, I am right with God and this being right does not come from my following the law. It comes from God through faith. God uses my faith in Christ to make me right with him. (Philippians 3:7–9 ICB)

The redemption of our dreams comes not in God's granting us our dreams but in our allowing God to make heaven's dreams our realities. We take our dreams back from the Enemy by taking back our rightful position as children of God. We go back to the childlike state of heart in which we recognized that the hunt was as much fun or more than the find.

God is at work at all times to bring about His dreams for us, and that means He's also working on the deeper issue of our character. When we understand this, we can lay hold of the dreams. When we start to shine forth His attributes, we begin to realize the dreams even before their full maturation. I was teaching Bible studies—or at least trying to—before I had an actual pulpit. I was walking in my role as Pastor Bob before I was officially Pastor Bob because I've always been Pastor Bob in God's plan. It works the same for each of us, and that's good reason for hope.

Time to Trust

It's all a matter of timing and trust. Believe it or not, we only need the part of the dream that God says we need when we need it, and not a minute before. God is setting each piece of the puzzle before us, one at a time. Learning to walk daily by faith in what God is doing presently in our lives is an exciting adventure.

Through Joseph's time of waiting for his dream to come true, his faith was fortified. Every minute of his journey had been carefully planned, perfectly orchestrated, and divinely chosen. After he interpreted Pharaoh's dream, Pharaoh gave Joseph charge over the entire kingdom of Egypt:

Turning to Joseph, Pharaoh said, "Since God has revealed the meaning of the dreams to you, you are the wisest man in the land! I hereby appoint you to direct this project. You will manage my household and organize all my people. Only I will have a rank higher than yours."

And Pharaoh said to Joseph, "I hereby put you in charge of the entire land of Egypt." Then Pharaoh placed his own signet ring on Joseph's finger as a symbol of his authority. He dressed him in beautiful clothing and placed the royal gold chain about his neck. Pharaoh also gave Joseph the chariot of his second-in-command, and wherever he went the command was shouted, "Kneel down!" So Joseph was put in charge of all Egypt. And Pharaoh said to Joseph, "I am the king, but no one will move a hand or a foot in the entire land of Egypt without your approval."

Pharaoh renamed him Zaphenath-paneah and gave him a wife— a young woman named Asenath, the daughter of Potiphera, priest of Heliopolis. So Joseph took charge of the entire land of Egypt. He was thirty years old when he entered the service of Pharaoh, the king of Egypt. And when Joseph left Pharaoh's presence, he made a tour of inspection throughout the land. (Genesis 41:39–46 NLT)

Let this sink in. Joseph went to bed one night as a prisoner, and the next day he was the second-highest-ranking dignitary in all of Egypt. He had a family, power, position, prestige—all at the age of thirty.

Had Joseph not stayed in step with God's plan, he would have settled for second best. The position with Potiphar was better than the pit, better than the marketplace, and better than the prison, but God wasn't leading him to "better." God always gives "best"—but in His timing.

What happened to Joseph was exactly what was supposed to happen in his life, and he came to understand that. When he was reunited with his brothers, and they feared he would take vengeance on them for what they had done to him years earlier, he told them, "You meant evil against me; but God meant it for good, in order to bring it about as it is this day, to save many people alive" (Genesis 50:20).

Notice that Joseph did not say that God worked out all those terrible things for good. He specifically said that God *meant* them for good. Joseph recognized God's sovereignty and His providential hand at work in his life. Because of Joseph's willingness to allow God to use him as He saw fit, many people's lives were spared.

Let me congratulate you on coming this far in your journey toward dreamality. You've made it through the pit, recognizing that your dream isn't really yours, and you can't make it happen. You've endured the marketplace, acknowledging God's sovereignty and the fact that He's the one who will have to fulfill your dream. You've even persevered through prison. And now, hopefully, you've begun to understand why it seems the dream is taking so long to come to pass. God is waiting to live out His dream through you. He's just wondering if you're willing to wait for His best rather than settling for something less. I hope you'll trust God's timing. Take it from me—heaven's dream is worth the wait.

Are you ready to put the last three pieces of the puzzle into place? In the next three chapters, we'll take a closer look at what God is able to do when we're willing to wait. If heaven's dreams for our lives include the provision to share, the power to save, and the position to shine, how then are these blessings manifested in our lives? God's work in us in these three areas will produce fruit. The provision to share will yield an abundant life. The power to save will cultivate a supernatural life. And the position to shine will display the excellence of life in Christ.

"Glory be to God! By his mighty power at work within us, he is able to accomplish infinitely more than we would ever dare to ask or hope" (Ephesians 3:20 NLT). God will do in us what we never could have dreamed possible.

an abundant *dream*

When we really get into God's Word, one thing becomes crystal clear: the difference between man's economy and God's economy is as stark as the difference between night and day. The world tells us we need to look out for number one; God tells us to esteem others more highly than ourselves. The world honors the most prestigious and powerful in position; God honors the humble. The world's strategy for success is to work our way up the ladder, stepping on as many people as necessary to get there; on God's ladder of success, it's not how high we go but how we treat others along the way—and some of us will be shocked to discover that the bottom is actually the top.

This contrast of worlds shows up brilliantly in the area of our provision to share. Many people have an abundance of stuff, but not all of them are walking in God's spiritual abundance. Jesus must have been talking about something beyond material goods when He said, "The thief does not come except to steal, and to kill, and to destroy. I have come that they may have life, and that they may have it more abundantly" (John 10:10). How then does the abundant life that comes with the God-given dream differ from living the self-driven dream?

The Paradox of Abundant Poverty

This distinction is found in the paradox of an abundant life that embraces poverty. Jesus gave us this insight when He taught, "Blessed are the poor in spirit, for theirs is the kingdom of heaven" (Matthew 5:3).

We often cringe at this beatitude and scratch our heads at the contradiction of terms because we have a skewed understanding of the word *poor*. People in the Western world spend their lives chasing the dream of health, wealth, and power. This fleshly fantasy has even become the mantra and foundational doctrine of some of our modern-day churches that teach that Jesus was wealthy and that we are "the King's kids." They tell us that if we aren't driving Rolls Royces, then something's wrong with our faith because as royalty we can command heaven to pour out the blessings that are rightfully ours.

This mind-set flies in the face of the gentle, meek, and lowly man from Nazareth who was born in a manger, had no place to lay His head or call home, and who even had to be buried in a borrowed tomb.

The biblical concept of poverty is quite different from our worldly understanding. God is a giver, and we were originally created in His image—to be givers. But we were infected through the Fall with a sin nature that made us takers instead. God uses resources to protect and bless others. We use resources to protect and bless ourselves. God continually pours Himself out for the sake of others. We continually hoard everything we can to avoid ever being in want.

Our sin nature has caused us to forget that we're hard-wired in the image of God. He designed us to find joy in giving, not having. With God less is more. It's the pattern Christ set for us: "You know the grace of our Lord Jesus Christ, that though he was rich, yet for your sakes he became poor, so that you through his poverty might become rich" (2 Corinthians 8:9 NIV). The abundance of heaven's dream is found as we become less and less ourselves—with our sinful nature—

and more and more conformed to the image of God, the ultimate Giver. That's what redemption is all about. It happens when we accept God's offer of salvation through Jesus Christ. As the Spirit of Christ inhabits our hearts through faith, our provision to share comes not out of the abundance of what we have but out of the abundance of who we are in Christ. We are once again givers, not takers, because the Giver lives in us and through us.

Consider this explanation from author and founder of the ministry Setting Captives Free, Mike Cleveland:

> Our God is continually pouring Himself out selflessly for us. Jesus's sacrifice on the cross was not the only time this happened. The Cross was the moment in time that this reality was made fully manifest for humanity to witness. Yet this self-sacrificing nature, this poverty-of-self, is an inherent part of who our God is. And to be empowered to walk in complete self-abandonment is to be empowered by the Spirit to walk just as He is. We cannot conjure this up from within ourselves. There is no spark within that can be kindled into a flame of selflessness. It is a divine substance of agape love that fuels the fires of self-poverty. It must be imparted by ingesting His nature at the table of feasting to which He calls us. Poverty-of-self will only be a trait in our lives as we die to self and are in full subjection to the sovereign rule of God. Only through death-to-self will the control of the Spirit of God evidence itself in our lives.[1]

Spiritual Wisdom versus Human Understanding

Until we embrace this idea of poverty of self by abandoning all self-driven efforts to make a dream happen in our lives, we won't experience the abundance of heaven's dream. When we try to make a dream happen in our own strength, we're operating from a self-centered base. Not only does that limit us to our own resources, but we'll also never be satisfied, because our human value system is contrary to God's value system, with which we are divinely hard-wired.

When the dream is God-given, however, it brings with it access to His infinite resources and a new way of thinking that incorporates God's value system. The Bible calls this a higher way of thinking and indicates that it's divine, not human, in origin: "As the heavens are higher than the earth, so are My ways higher than your ways, and My thoughts than your thoughts" (Isaiah 55:9).

In Christ we find a wisdom that is beyond street smarts, business savvy, and common sense. Sure, we admire people who are street smart. We respect those who know which stocks to buy, what investments to make, and how to bring in the most profit. We look up to people who instinctively know what to do in a given situation. But there is a kind of intelligence, knowledge, and wisdom that transcends all these other types of intelligence: spiritual wisdom. This kind of wisdom is only for those who have matured into their God-given dreams. Those who are still walking in their own self-driven dreams cannot understand it, as the apostle Paul explained:

> *We do, however, speak a message of wisdom among the mature, but not the wisdom of this age or of the rulers of this age, who are coming to nothing. No, we speak of God's secret wisdom, a wisdom that has been hidden and that God destined for our glory before time began. None of the rulers of this age understood it, for if they had, they would not have crucified the Lord of glory. However, as it is written: "No eye has seen, no ear has heard, no mind has conceived what God has prepared for those who love him"—but God has revealed it to us by his Spirit.*
>
> *The Spirit searches all things, even the deep things of God. . . . The man without the Spirit does not accept the things that come from the Spirit of God, for they are foolishness to him, and he cannot understand them, because they are spiritually discerned. (1 Corinthians 2:6–10, 14 NIV)*

We see then that there are basically two kinds of people. The first group includes those who have accepted God's plan for their lives and have His wisdom. They recognize the value and worth of spiritual things. They embrace the principles and concepts I've shared and understand how they impact their dreams.

The second group includes critics who are simply curious about the things of God. Such "natural" people live without the Spirit of God. They don't see the great value of spiritual things. For them, a worship service is just a time for singing songs. For them, this book has too many Bible verses in it, and they're not completely comfortable with the direction it seems to be taking.

> In Christ we find a wisdom that is beyond street smarts, business savvy, and common sense.

We see the dissimilarity of these two groups manifested most in their attitudes toward spiritual things. Take baptism, for instance. The natural person sees a group of people show up at a beach. They go into the water one at a time, and someone dunks them under water and brings them back up. They leave the water overjoyed, apparently experiencing some kind of high that makes the natural person wonder if there's some drug in that part of the water that's being absorbed through the skin. He or she can't fathom what could possibly be the difference between those being dunked and another group at the beach for a family outing. The natural person sees the family going in and out of that same water, and yet nothing is happening to them.

Those who are spiritual say, "Of course nothing is happening to the other group. They're not publicly proclaiming their faith in Christ. They're just enjoying a day at the beach." It takes spiritual discernment to perceive why there's a difference. The Bible says that without the

Spirit of God, spiritual things seem somewhat foolish: "The man without the Spirit does not accept the things that come from the Spirit of God, for they are foolishness to him, and he cannot understand them, because they are spiritually discerned" (1 Corinthians 2:14 NIV). Though a person without God's Spirit could comprehend the physical practices of baptism, communion, and other such religious rites, he or she cannot grasp the depth of their meaning because they only become meaningful when the Spirit of God enlightens hearts and minds to understand their importance.

To the person without divine wisdom, communion can seem illogical. The natural person might think, *Why don't they get a big mug instead of those silly little cups? Why don't they get some real food, or at least a bigger chunk of bread?* People think this because they don't get it. They cannot comprehend that it's not the size of the cup, it's the spirit of the moment that makes this more than a meal.

This disparity between natural and spiritual people is nothing new. The difference has been clear almost from day one. Abel was spiritual; Cain was not. For the life of him, Cain could not figure out why God accepted Abel's offering but not his. His lack of spiritual understanding made him miss the whole point of the sacrifice in the first place and drove him mad enough to murder his brother.

John the Baptist didn't fit the religious-leader mold of his day. Even though his role was the important one of announcing and preparing the way for Jesus Christ, the long-awaited Messiah and King, John didn't wear the long robes or act like the religious leaders of his day. He wore a camel's-hair tunic; he ate locusts and honey and lived in the wilderness (see Matthew 3:4). So picture the scene—a man wearing animal skins with wild, matted hair, eating bugs—he's supposed to be God's representative? Are you serious? He's wild! He can't possibly know God.

That was the natural person's way of looking at John the Baptist, and it's the same for the natural mind of today. We stumble over nonconforming personalities because we've been conditioned to expect that everyone who knows God will look and act a certain way. If the person fits our stereotype, we can believe he or she is from God. But there's no way this wild guy, John the Baptist, or other unorthodox characters could be from God—not in the eyes of the natural person.

This human propensity to look at things from the natural viewpoint caused people in Christ's day to miss the Messiah. They looked at Jesus and thought, *That guy? He can't be the Messiah. That's Mary's boy. I grew up down the road from him. I used to see him hanging around Joseph's workshop. He's not the Messiah. Don't even go there.*

They were devoid of the wisdom of God that would allow them to see what was really happening in Jesus's ministry and at His crucifixion. As the Author of life hung on the cross, they mocked Him: "Let Him save Himself if He is the Christ, the chosen of God" (Luke 23:35). They missed it. It took the earthquake and a solar blackout before some were willing to admit that He might be the Son of God. Even then they promptly put their brief moment of belief behind them because in their own wisdom they concluded that if Jesus were God, surely He would have saved Himself from death on the cross. They were so spiritually dull that they didn't even realize He could have saved Himself but chose not to so He could save us.

The spiritually minded and naturally minded also part ways when it comes to understanding our dreams. When we tell those who have natural minds about our God-given dreams, we shouldn't expect them to jump on our bandwagons. When we say to a naturally minded individual, "I'm going to church instead of happy hour," we can anticipate criticism or cajoling. Or when we say, "I've been living with my boyfriend for two years, but we've both made a commitment to Christ, and now we've decided to live separately until we pledge our lives to each other in marriage," we can count on jaws dropping.

Fort Lauderdale has its share of people living together. Our counselors can recall many sessions during which unmarried couples have made the difficult decision to honor God with their lives and move into separate residences until they're married. Unfortunately, other people never get it. With their natural minds, they can't understand God's wisdom when the Bible declares, "Among you there must not be even a hint of sexual immorality, or of any kind of impurity, or of greed, because these are improper for God's holy people" (Ephesians 5:3 NIV). Holy living seems so antiquated, absurd, prudish, and economically unsound. But to those who have received the wisdom of God through the Spirit of God, the principles of Scripture are life-giving truths that make perfect, mature sense and produce divine results.

Why do I belabor the point of spiritual wisdom? I have to in order to connect the dots between this wisdom and the abundance of a God-given dream. God will not bestow His abundance on a person who doesn't have the wisdom to know what to do with it.

> Only when we've received the spiritual wisdom of God can we be trusted with the abundance inherent in our God-given dreams.

Let's conduct a hypothetical experiment. If we were to equally redistribute all of the world's wealth among the population, how long would it be before the greedy and more aggressive members of society took advantage of those with less power? The Bible hints at the answer by explaining the cause of that behavior:

Do you know where your fights and arguments come from? They come from the selfish desires that make war inside you. You want things, but you do not have them. So you are ready to kill and are jealous of other people. But you still cannot get what you want. So you argue and fight. You do not get what you want because you do not ask God. Or when you ask, you do not receive because the reason you ask is wrong. You want things only so that you can use them for your own pleasures. (James 4:1–3 ICB)

It's not a pretty picture, but it's an accurate one.

The human race is in dire need of redemption, and so are our dreams. This is especially true when we consider the abundance heaven's dreams will always bring. God wants to entrust us with His resources, but He must first make sure we have developed the spiritual wisdom that originates from Him. That wisdom is described this way: "The wisdom that comes from God is like this: First, it is pure. Then it is also peaceful, gentle, and easy to please. This wisdom is always ready to help those who are troubled and to do good for others. This wisdom is always fair and honest" (James 3:17 ICB). Only when we've received the spiritual wisdom of God can we be trusted with the abundance inherent in our God-given dreams.

The Rewards of Spiritual Wisdom

God's wisdom is peaceful and gentle, ready to help others and do good, and it's always fair and honest. These qualities place spiritual wisdom worlds above human wisdom. Is it any wonder that many times God has to take us through the pit, the marketplace, and the prison to develop this kind of wisdom? They're part of the maturing process the apostle Paul wrote about in Ephesians 4:13: "We must become like a mature person—we must grow until we become like Christ and have all his perfection" (ICB). Only as we learn the lessons of those training grounds will we embrace the poverty of self, the self-sacrificing nature. John the Baptist alluded to the kind of growth we need in order to be perfected in Christ when he said of Jesus, "He must increase, but I must decrease" (John 3:30). Only then can we shine forth the fullness of God and His wisdom.

This is another way of looking at poverty of self. The less the world can see of us, the more they will see of Jesus. Sanctification is not a process through which we become like Jesus by our own efforts. It's a process whereby we get out of the way and allow Jesus to live through us. The Bible describes this as dying to ourselves. Jesus put it this way: "If anyone wants to follow me, he must say 'no' to the things he wants. Every day he must be willing even to die on a cross, and he must follow me" (Luke 9:23 ICB).

In our own flesh, we'll never be mature enough to handle the responsibilities that accompany a God-given dream. The apostle Paul realized this human limitation and stated it this way:

> *I know I am rotten through and through so far as my old sinful nature is concerned. No matter which way I turn, I can't make myself do right. I want to, but I can't. When I want to do good, I don't. And when I try not to do wrong, I do it anyway. But if I am doing what I don't want to do, I am not really the one doing it; the sin within me is doing it.*
>
> *It seems to be a fact of life that when I want to do what is right, I inevitably do what is wrong. I love God's law with all my heart. But there is another law at work within me that is at war with my mind. This law wins the fight and makes me a slave to the sin that is still within me. Oh, what a miserable person I am! Who will free me from this life that is dominated by sin? Thank God! The answer is in Jesus Christ our Lord. (Romans 7:18–25 NLT)*

Only in Christ are we capable of doing what is peaceful, right, good, fair, and honest to help others. Therefore, God cannot entrust us with the responsibility of abundance until He has empowered us with maturity in Christ. If He did, it would be as irresponsible as a parent giving an eleven-year-old the keys to the car and house and then going on vacation for two weeks. We're appalled at the idea because we know that an eleven-year-old isn't ready to handle that degree of responsibility.

Joseph had to mature in wisdom before he was ready for the degree of responsibility that living out his God-given dream involved. At the beginning of his story we saw what seemed like a slightly cocky teenager, flaunting his dream in front of his already jealous brothers. After enduring the pit, the marketplace, and the prison, Joseph emerged with a wisdom that could see the beauty of the lessons learned in the pit, the clarification of the dream in the marketplace, and the goodness of God in spite of the prison. He was finally ready for the responsibility of heaven's dream. And it was this godly wisdom that paved the way for the dream to be fulfilled: "Pharaoh said to Joseph, 'Inasmuch as God has shown you all this, there is no one as discerning and wise as you. You shall be over my house, and all my people shall be ruled according to your word; only in regard to the throne will I be greater than you'" (Genesis 41:39–40).

Joseph had gained a heart of understanding and wisdom that put him in a place where God could orchestrate through him a plan that provided not only for himself, his family, and Pharaoh's household, but for all of Egypt, Israel, and the surrounding countries:

When all Egypt began to feel the famine, the people cried to Pharaoh for food. Then Pharaoh told all the Egyptians, "Go to Joseph and do what he tells you."

When the famine had spread over the whole country, Joseph opened the storehouses and sold grain to the Egyptians, for the famine was severe throughout Egypt. And all the countries came to Egypt to buy grain from Joseph, because the famine was severe in all the world. (Genesis 41:55–57 NIV)

The Consequence of Spiritual Immaturity

What happens if we don't mature? What if we never grow in our relationship with God? We find the answer to this question in the interesting contrast between Joseph and his brothers. Joseph had undergone great injustice at the hands of his siblings, and yet the tide turned dramatically at this point in the journey. Whereas the brothers walked away from the pit, never had to experience the marketplace, and escaped the bars of prison, they also never matured in their relationship with God, perhaps because they never gained the spiritual wisdom that comes from these testing grounds. As Joseph's dream was coming true, his brothers were still stuck in their self-driven dreams and so devoid of wisdom that their father had to tell them what to do: "Jacob learned that there was grain in Egypt. So he said to his sons, 'Why are you just sitting here looking at one another? I have heard that there is grain in Egypt. Go down there and buy grain for us to eat. Then we will live and not die'" (Genesis 42:1–2 ICB).

I can picture this hilarious scene. No one has any food to eat. Everyone is pretty hungry, which means they're probably pretty grouchy too. Finally Jacob looks at this group of grown men and, in an irritated tone, says, "Why are you just sitting around looking at each other?" They didn't even have the initiative to get help when they were in danger of starving to death.

The contrast between Joseph and his brothers highlights how important it is for all believers to pursue a path of spiritual growth, discovering the abundance that is ours in Christ. Without this knowledge we will never see heaven's dreams become realities in our lives. It's one thing to squander worldly abundance on personal satisfaction. It's quite another to be unaware of the spiritual abundance God makes available. Spiritual ignorance is directly related to and responsible for spiritual immaturity. It typically manifests itself in three ways: ignorance of our condition, ignorance of our calling, and ignorance of our destiny.

Ignorance of Our Condition

Many people in churches today are like Joseph's brothers. They're part of the family of God, but they don't know where to find God's provision. They sit around looking at one another and don't have a clue as to where they can find the sustenance that will fill their hungry souls. They're stuck because they've looked at their lives with natural eyes and failed to grasp the inadequacy of their own power. They think that just because they go to church every week, pay their pound of flesh in donations or volunteer work, and have a devotional reading each morning that they are rich and well fed. Their lack of passion for Christ and compassion for others doesn't even concern them. And we can spot them a mile away because they lack joy and enthusiasm for life. Murmuring and complaining, they find fault with nearly everything. Their membership fees for Critics for Christ are paid up years in advance.

They're in the same boat with the clueless church of Laodicea that Jesus addressed in the book of Revelation:

> *Write this letter to the angel of the church in Laodicea. This is the message from the one who is the Amen—the faithful and true witness, the ruler of God's creation: I know all the things you do, that you are neither hot nor cold. I wish you were one or the other! But since you are like lukewarm water, I will spit you out of my mouth! You say, "I am rich. I have everything I want. I don't need a thing!" And you don't realize that you are wretched and miserable and poor and blind and naked. (Revelation 3:14–17 NLT)*

Lukewarm is not quite the description I think of when I ponder the abundant life. *Lukewarm* better describes a mediocre, bland life. That kind of life brings no glory to God. No wonder He wants to spit such believers out of His mouth.

Perhaps you've had the experience of being served a meal in a restaurant that looks appetizing, yet when you take a bite, it's like a tasteless wad of lard. It fills your mouth to the point of gagging you, and in spite of not wanting to be rude, you have to spit it out before you throw up.

That's God's response toward believers who live halfhearted lives. The Lord is disgusted and repulsed by the lifeless, tasteless experience too many believers have resigned themselves to in His name. And why wouldn't He be when we consider all that belongs to us in Christ, yet we live as if we never really knew Him?

Ignorance of Our Calling

In his epistle to the Ephesian church, Paul addressed some believers' propensity to stagnate and live beneath God's level of provision. After three chapters of describing all that God has done for us, Paul concludes in chapter 4: "I urge you to live a life worthy of the calling you have received" (Ephesians 4:1 NIV).

As Christians we must live worthy of our calling. What calling? It's outlined in this same epistle:

In Christ, God has given us every spiritual blessing in heaven. In Christ, he chose us before the world was made. In his love he chose us to be his holy people—people without blame before him. And before the world was made, God decided to make us his own children through Jesus Christ. That was what he wanted and what pleased him. This brings praise to God because of his wonderful grace. God gave that grace to us freely, in Christ, the One he loves. In Christ we are set free by the blood of his death. And so we have forgiveness of sins because of God's rich grace. . . .

In Christ we were chosen to be God's people. . . .

I pray that you will know that the blessings God has promised his holy people are rich and glorious. And you will know that God's power is very great for us who believe. That power is the same as the great strength God used to raise Christ from death and put him at his right side in heaven. . . .

We were spiritually dead because of the things we did wrong against God. But God gave us new life with Christ. You have been saved by God's grace. And he raised us up with Christ and gave us a

seat with him in the heavens. He did this for those of us who are in
Christ Jesus. . . .

Yes, at one time you were far away from God. But now in Christ
Jesus you are brought near to God through the blood of Christ's death.
Because of Christ we now have peace. . . .

Yes, through Christ we all have the right to come to the Father in
one Spirit. . . .

In Christ we can come before God with freedom and without fear.
We can do this through faith in Christ. . . .

Christ's love is greater than any person can ever know. But I pray
that you will be able to know that love. Then you can be filled with the
fullness of God.

With God's power working in us, God can do much, much more
than anything we can ask or think of. (Ephesians 1:3–7, 11, 18–20,
2:5–6, 13–14, 18, 3:12, 19–20 ICB)

In Christ we have been chosen by God, forgiven of our sins and
saved from sin itself, given every spiritual blessing, made a part of God's
family, given new life, and imbued with the same power God used to
raise Christ from the dead so that we can do "much, much more than
anything we can ask or think of." Now we can see why God finds it so
despicable when we possess all this wealth and abundance and yet live as
paupers. Not only do we rob ourselves of what is our rightful inheritance
in Christ, but we also paint a very undesirable picture for the world
around us of who God is.

God is not boring, nor is He broke. Yet if we look at a lot of
churches in our world today, that's exactly how He's represented. He's
made to look broke because all they talk about is money, which is part
of what makes Him seem so boring. I'm just an average guy, but my life
is way more exciting than the life in God as portrayed by many
churches. I would be highly offended if people talked about me the way
they speak about Him.

Ignorance of Our Destiny

How do we sink from the abundance of what God's calling offers to the emptiness of a mundane life? We get there because we would rather settle for a humdrum existence than let get and embark on the adventure of faith for which God has destined us. That's why Jesus warned us, "Whoever desires to save his life will lose it, but whoever loses his life for My sake and the gospel's will save it" (Mark 8:35).

What happens if we lose our lives? What if we really let go? The Bible tells us, "To everyone who has, more will be given, and he will have abundance; but from him who does not have, even what he has will be taken away" (Matthew 25:29). The Greek term for abundance (*perisseúo*) means "to superabound." In other words, God's plan for our lives is beyond measure. If we let go of what we can measure, we will be in a position to receive the immeasurable superabundance of all that God has. This makes perfect sense when we consider that we are finite beings, but God is infinite. Therefore, as we follow John the Baptist's example and decrease so that Christ can increase, our limits give way to His infinite ability.

Remember from chapter 2 that God is spirit, and He operates above our natural realm. God is not just superhuman; He's supernatural. This means that in Christ, we also will function in a realm outside of the natural. That's how Moses parted the Red Sea and Peter walked on water. It's how Paul was able to heal the sick. And it's how God orchestrates His dream through us. In the next chapter, we'll look more fully at this supernatural aspect of heaven's dreams.

a supernatural *dream*

When I mention the words *supernatural* or *miracle*, what comes to mind? Do you think of someone being healed of cancer? Do you think of the parting of the Red Sea, the feeding of the five thousand, or a vision of the Blessed Mother? Our understanding of the supernatural realm is as diverse as our backgrounds. Since heaven's dreams have the power to save because of their supernatural quality, it will be helpful to define our terms.

A Miracle Defined

One theologian offered the following definition of *miracle*, based on the three different Greek words (in parentheses) translated "miracle" in the New Testament: "A miracle is an unusual and significant event (*terasa*) which requires the working of a supernatural agent (*dunamis*) and is performed for the purpose of authenticating the message or the messenger (*semeion*)."[1]

If we apply this definition to our subject of God-given dreams, we can deduce that God wants to perform an unusual and significant event that will require a supernatural agent for the purpose of authenticating the message or messenger. We may not experience the same degree of unusual and significant events as did Moses, Elijah, the apostles, or Jesus, but one of the surefire earmarks of God's hand on us is some sort of supernatural authentication.

The apostle Peter wrote, "You are a chosen people, a royal priesthood, a holy nation, a people belonging to God, that you may declare the praises of him who called you out of darkness into his wonderful light" (1 Peter 2:9 NIV). In the King James Version, "a people belonging to God" is rendered "a peculiar people." When we're walking in God's plans for our lives, we're different from other people in this world. That difference is seen in how we think—as we saw in chapter 10—and in whom we belong to and how that ownership manifests itself in our lives. We belong to God—to a supernatural God. That means that supernatural events will be part of our lives.

This is hard for many people to acknowledge because we've been programmed by our culture to consider only those things that are beyond the scope of human experience or understanding to be miracles. Yet approximately eleven thousand miracles occur every day in the United States in the form of new babies entering the world.[2]

One might argue that babies aren't really miracles, but let's apply our definition. The birth of a child is an unusual and significant event requiring a supernatural agent for the purpose of establishing the message or messenger. Think something occurring eleven thousand times a day is not unusual? Tell that to first-time parents. No one would deny the unique experience and significance of having a child. Wondering what the supernatural agent might be? In the Bible the psalmist tells us God is: "You made all the delicate, inner parts of my body and knit me together in my mother's womb" (Psalm 139:13 NLT). And what would be the message?

Some people are still frantically hunting for the missing link, that theoretical primate postulated to bridge the evolutionary gap between anthropoid apes and human beings. But I believe, in this day and age of DNA, that we have to resign ourselves to the fact that God is the Author of life. As scientists study the complex design of DNA molecules, it becomes increasingly difficult to attribute life to the random process of evolution. Each tiny strand of DNA is not a chance product but one of intelligent design. That's the message God authenticates every time a precious, tiny bundle of joy is born. Yet because birth is a miracle that happens daily, it's easy to overlook its truly miraculous nature.

> Because of the ordinary way in which God chooses to work in and through the lives of those with a God-given dream, many times His miracles go undetected by the natural eye.

In the same way, because of the ordinary way in which God chooses to work in and through the lives of those with a God-given dream, many times His miracles go undetected by the natural eye. That's what happened to Balaam, as we see in Numbers 22.

The story begins when the children of Israel, nearing the end of their journey to the Promised Land, camped on the plains of Moab. Balak, king of the Moabites, greatly feared the Israelites because they had soundly defeated another local people, the Amorites, in battle. In a desperate effort to protect his land and people from Israel's invading hordes, Balak sent for Balaam to help him.

God spoke to Balaam and told him that he was not to go and curse Israel, so in obedience Balaam initially refused. But when Balak upped the ante, offering more prestige and reward if Balaam would comply, Balaam began to waver. He invited the envoys to stay the night so he could ask the Lord again for permission to go with them. In what seems to be a concession, God told Balaam he could go with the men from

Moab but must only speak what the Lord told him to say concerning the children of Israel.

The Bible tells us next that the Lord's anger was aroused because Balaam went with the men. This seems odd at first because God told Balaam he could go with them. But when we consider the story from the perspective of a parent, it comes into clearer view. We often give our children choices because we hope they'll make the right one. It's disappointing and frustrating to see them make wrong choices when they clearly know our hearts on an issue.

Balaam knew full well that God did not want him to go with the men from Moab. He knew God would never curse His own people. In 2 Peter 2:15 and Jude 1:11, we're told the reason Balaam overrode God's wisdom: greed. God tried to spare him from the consequences of a costly mistake by making Balaam's donkey refuse to go into the path of the Angel of the Lord, who would have killed Balaam. Unfortunately, Balaam was so blinded by his greed that he failed to see God's hand until God blatantly revealed it:

Balaam rose in the morning, saddled his donkey, and went with the princes of Moab.

Then God's anger was aroused because he went, and the Angel of the Lord took His stand in the way as an adversary against him. And he was riding on his donkey, and his two servants were with him. Now the donkey saw the Angel of the Lord standing in the way with His drawn sword in His hand, and the donkey turned aside out of the way and went into the field. So Balaam struck the donkey to turn her back onto the road. Then the Angel of the Lord stood in a narrow path between the vineyards, with a wall on this side and a wall on that side. And when the donkey saw the Angel of the Lord, she pushed herself against the wall and crushed Balaam's foot against the wall; so he struck her again. Then the Angel of the Lord went further, and stood in a

narrow place where there was no way to turn either to the right hand
or to the left. And when the donkey saw the Angel of the LORD, she lay
down under Balaam; so Balaam's anger was aroused, and he struck the
donkey with his staff.

Then the LORD opened the mouth of the donkey, and she said to
Balaam, "What have I done to you, that you have struck me these three
times?"

And Balaam said to the donkey, "Because you have abused me. I
wish there were a sword in my hand, for now I would kill you!"

So the donkey said to Balaam, "Am I not your donkey on which you
have ridden, ever since I became yours, to this day? Was I ever disposed
to do this to you?"

And he said, "No."

Then the LORD opened Balaam's eyes, and he saw the Angel of the
LORD standing in the way with His drawn sword in His hand; and he
bowed his head and fell flat on his face. And the Angel of the LORD said
to him, "Why have you struck your donkey these three times? Behold, I
have come out to stand against you, because your way is perverse before
Me. The donkey saw Me and turned aside from Me these three times.
If she had not turned aside from Me, surely I would also have killed you
by now, and let her live."

And Balaam said to the Angel of the LORD, "I have sinned, for I
did not know You stood in the way against me. Now therefore, if it dis-
pleases You, I will turn back."

Then the Angel of the LORD said to Balaam, "Go with the men,
but only the word that I speak to you, that you shall speak." So Balaam
went with the princes of Balak. (Numbers 22:21–35)

I don't know if I find it more astounding that the donkey talked to
Balaam or that Balaam talked back without a second thought! Either
way, most people looking at this passage of Scripture would say that the

miraculous event was the donkey's talking. Yet it was just part of the miracle. The unusual and significant event requiring a supernatural agent for the purpose of authenticating the message wasn't just the donkey's talking but also the donkey's refusal to proceed. The Angel of the Lord was the supernatural agent, and the message was authenticated by the donkey's ability to speak. However, it wasn't the donkey's ability to speak that spared Balaam's life but rather the donkey's ability to see the Angel of the Lord and turn away.

It's noteworthy how naturally the miraculous intrudes into everyday life. Balaam never blinked twice or seemed surprised because that miracle manifested itself in an entirely natural sequence of events. The donkey seemed unruly, crushing Balaam's foot against a wall. It was so natural that in spite of her talking, Balaam didn't comprehend what was happening until God opened his eyes to see the Angel of the Lord and the danger that would have befallen him had he continued on his path.

As we discovered earlier in this book, the Bible reveals the existence of two parallel realms—one we can see and one we can't. If we're going to walk in the supernatural dynamic of our dreams, we must equip ourselves with the necessary tools to see past the physical into the spiritual. Otherwise, God may have to use a talking donkey to get our attention!

A Practical Faith

We've discussed faith a great deal throughout this book, so by now we understand that it's faith that enables us to see the unseen. That's why in this chapter I want to get really practical about how we build our faith. The Bible tells us, "Faith comes by hearing, and hearing by the word of God" (Romans 10:17). Faith doesn't necessarily come by the kind of physical hearing we do with our ears. If it did, everyone who ever heard of God would believe in Him. But everyone doesn't. Therefore we must consider not just the first half of the verse (faith comes by hearing) but the second half as well (hearing comes by the

Word of God). The kind of hearing that produces faith is cultivated through reading God's Word.

The Bible is God's manual for mankind. He created us, and He gave us instructions for life: "All Scripture is inspired by God and is useful to teach us what is true and to make us realize what is wrong in our lives. It straightens us out and teaches us to do what is right" (2 Timothy 3:16 NLT).

Much like we have instruction manuals for our automobiles, we also have one for living. We can ignore the vehicle manual and put water in the gas tank instead of gasoline. That's our prerogative. We could even argue that water is better than gas because it costs less, smells better, and is more environmentally friendly. But it won't be long before we find out that the

> God gave us His Word because it has everything we need to live at our highest potential and for our ultimate best interest.

manufacturer knew which of the two would give the best performance.

God knows how humanity functions best. We can argue against His Word and demand our right to choose, but the jury is already in on the result of sinful living. God gave us His Word because it has everything we need to live at our highest potential and for our ultimate best interest. For example, though it runs contrary to society's prevailing attitudes, the Bible tells us not to have sexual relationships outside the safety and commitment of marriage. God isn't trying to ruin our fun or hinder our freedom. He's letting us know that we were designed for monogamous relationships built on trust and caring. Anything less will have disastrous results. This is just one instruction from our Creator, but the principle is that God's Word applies in every aspect of life so that we can live life to the fullest.

How does this principle pertain to faith? As we accept God's plans for our lives—exchanging our own lives for His—we receive the gift of God's Spirit residing within us. The Spirit then illuminates God's Word to us.

The Bible never made sense to me as a nonbeliever. I read but could not for the life of me understand what I was reading. After I received Christ, through a conscious decision to exchange my life for His, I supernaturally had the ability to understand what I was reading. I also began to feel a new desire to live in a way that would please God. As I read the Bible, I found clear direction on how to do that. The more I walked in obedience to what I was learning, the more my life began to take on a supernatural dynamic, and I could see God's hand moving in my day-to-day circumstances. After a while it became so obvious that God was orchestrating matters that I stopped calling things coincidences and began referring to them as "God-o-inces."

I want to emphasize that this supernatural dynamic wasn't spooky or scary. It was something quite natural. I would end up in the right place at the right time. I'd bump into someone I had been praying for. I would know in the deepest part of my understanding things about people I was counseling that I had no way of knowing. Scriptures would pop into my mind pertaining to situations I encountered. And I grew in my understanding of God's Word and in my appreciation for His ways.

The Bible makes many references to many stages of Christian growth. It speaks of babies who need the milk of the Word (see 1 Peter 2:2), young men who are walking strong in the Word (see 1 John 2:13), and fathers of the faith who are training others in the Word (see 1 Thessalonians 2:11; 1 Timothy 3:2; 2 Timothy 2:2; 1 Peter 5:1–3). The common factor in all stages of spiritual growth is God's Word. It's through the Word of God that we develop our faith, gain the wisdom of God, and discover the wealth of God's promises.

The spiritual person understands the value of God's Word, but the person without God's Spirit considers it simply a book with limited or no value for life. Yet the pages of this Book are filled with the promises through which God works the miracles that become dynamic parts of our everyday lives as Christians.

Consider just a few of these amazing statements the Bible makes about us when we're following God's paths and plans for our lives:

- *"The LORD will work out his plans for my life—for your faithful love, O LORD, endures forever."* (Psalm 138:8 NLT)

- *"You keep your loving promise. You lead the people you have saved. With your strength you will guide them to your holy land."* (Exodus 15:13 ICB)

- *"God causes everything to work together for the good of those who love God and are called according to his purpose for them."* (Romans 8:28 NLT)

- *"The Lord said to me, 'My grace is enough for you. When you are weak, then my power is made perfect in you.'"* (2 Corinthians 12:9 ICB)

- *"It is not that we think we can do anything of lasting value by ourselves. Our only power and success come from God."* (2 Corinthians 3:5 NLT)

- *"I can do all things through Christ who strengthens me."* (Philippians 4:13)

- *"I am sure that God, who began the good work within you, will continue his work until it is finally finished on that day when Christ Jesus comes back again."* (Philippians 1:6 NLT)

As we read these promises, we begin to see that God is working in and through us, and a strange thing begins to happen. The more we read the Word, the more we believe that God really can and will do what He said He would. That's how faith comes by hearing God's Word. And as our faith grows, our dreams appear more and more possible.

As long as we're looking at our own resources for making our dreams come true, we'll be convinced that they can't. We confirm this when we spend every ounce of energy, effort, and human ingenuity trying to accomplish what can only be done through God's supernatural power. We end up exhausted, despairing, and on the verge of quitting.

God's Divine Sufficiency

The real beauty of heaven's dreams becoming our realities is that when we have been purified in the pit, been perfected in the marketplace, persevered through prison, gained the wisdom for abundance, and begun to walk in the faith of God's promises, realizing our dreams becomes effortless.

It's easy to distinguish between those who are walking in heaven's dreams and those who are still striving for self-driven dreams. It's like the difference between someone who is gifted by God to sing and someone who has taken voice lessons all his or her life to try to hit the notes properly. The God-gifted singer is able to present that gift with ease and perfection. The self-made singer has to strive to perform similarly, and it still isn't as inspired or perfect as the performance by the person who is supernaturally gifted.

Heaven's dreams for our lives will be so remarkably distinct and effortless that they will make others look on and wonder how we do it. It looks so easy because God is working in us to accomplish it. All we must do is be available. God does the rest.

When someone who does not know the Lord has an amazing gift, I often hear Christians say things like, "Wow, if so-and-so got saved, can you imagine what God could do with all that talent?" That's typical of the human mind-set—and contrary to the truth about God. God doesn't need our talent, just our willingness to do whatever He asks.

John 6:1–14 tells about a boy with five loaves of bread and two fish. Jesus had been teaching a multitude of people and wanted to feed them. (Although this incident is known as the feeding of the five thousand,

Bible scholars estimate that the crowd was around ten thousand or more once women and children, who were not officially counted, are added in.) This kid had come with basically just enough food for himself, but he offered it to the Lord. In a sense he said, "This is all I have, but do whatever you want with it." Jesus took the lunch of one young boy and fed the entire crowd—and there were twelve baskets of food left over! God used a very natural thing, a boy's lunch, to accomplish a supernatural feat, feeding a multitude.

God can multiply resources, opportunities, and results beyond what we are humanly able to do, but we must place our dreams in the Master's hands. As long as we keep our eyes on our own capacities, abilities, or resources, we will continue to think, *I'm unable. I don't have enough. It'll never happen.* But in the hands of an infinite, sovereign God, our dreams can become realities.

Once, after a fellow pastor spoke as a guest in our church, he asked, "Bob, do you look once in a while at what God is doing here and say, 'Wow!'?" Without hesitation I replied, "No. Not once in a while but in every single service." I sincerely cannot, to this day, get over what God has done in my life. This is not what I asked for. It's more than I ever dreamed for my own life. Even now, if for one moment I look at my own resources, I feel overwhelmed at the prospect of pastoring a megachurch. Yet when I stay immersed in God's Word, my faith is built up, and I begin to look with excitement at even more things God can do. When I operate in God's supernatural strength, I don't feel weary in the work of the ministry; I feel energized and ready to take on the world for Jesus.

Our Human Inadequacy

Had Joseph not arrived at this place of seeing God's ability instead of his own, I truly believe he would have panicked when Pharaoh turned to him and said, "Hey, you're the man! You interpreted the dream, you had the solution, so you carry it out." Joseph easily could have looked at himself and thought, *I've never taken a course in business or property management. I can't do this!* We don't find this in Scripture because it didn't happen.

We do get a sense of human inadequacy in Joseph's brothers, however. They never quite seemed equal to the task they faced. They were probably sitting around looking at one another during the famine because they considered only the options presented by their own paltry resources. After getting grain from Egypt, when Joseph put their money back into their sacks, they scrambled to figure out how they, in their own abilities, should handle that turn of events. As we read this account, we can see how futile their own efforts appear and how blind they were to God's working, even to the point where they blamed Him for their situation:

> *Joseph gave a command to fill their sacks with grain, to restore every man's money to his sack, and to give them provisions for the journey. Thus he did for them. So they loaded their donkeys with the grain and departed from there. But as one of them opened his sack to give his donkey feed at the encampment, he saw his money; and there it was, in the mouth of his sack. So he said to his brothers, "My money has been restored, and there it is, in my sack!" Then their hearts failed them and they were afraid, saying to one another, "What is this that God has done to us?"*
>
> *Then they went to Jacob their father in the land of Canaan and told him all that had happened to them, saying: "The man who is lord of the land spoke roughly to us, and took us for spies of the country. But we said to him, 'We are honest men; we are not spies. We are twelve brothers, sons of our father; one is no more, and the youngest is with our father this day in the land of Canaan.' Then the man, the lord of the country, said to us, 'By this I will know that you are honest men: Leave one of your brothers here with me, take food for the famine of your households, and be gone. And bring your youngest brother to me; so I shall know that you are not spies, but that you are honest men. I will grant your brother to you, and you may trade in the land.'"*

Then it happened as they emptied their sacks, that surprisingly each man's bundle of money was in his sack; and when they and their father saw the bundles of money, they were afraid. And Jacob their father said to them, "You have bereaved me: Joseph is no more, Simeon is no more, and you want to take Benjamin. All these things are against me."

Then Reuben spoke to his father, saying, "Kill my two sons if I do not bring him back to you; put him in my hands, and I will bring him back to you."

But he said, "My son shall not go down with you, for his brother is dead, and he is left alone. If any calamity should befall him along the way in which you go, then you would bring down my gray hair with sorrow to the grave." (Genesis 42:25–38)

From a natural perspective, Joseph's brothers seem to have had better lives than Joseph did. They didn't have to go through the pit, the marketplace, or the prison. Yet in the moment of truth, when the rubber met the road and trusting God was vital, they were weighed in the balance and found wanting. They were unable to see God's hand in their circumstances, and as a sad result, they could save no one—not even themselves.

Were we sitting as unbelievers in the camp of Jacob at that time, we might be thinking, *Wow, these guys are no different from anyone else in the world. I thought their God was supposed to take care of them. I thought He was supposed to be supernatural. Even they don't seem to believe He'll come through for them.* In this case, the sons of Israel would not quite qualify as the "peculiar" people God's children are called to be.

The Miraculous Witness

Because it's human nature to panic when the going gets rough, there's no greater testimony of the miraculous in believers' lives than when we traverse our trials in perfect peace. It takes a supernatural ability to maintain a mind-set of trust in the midst of trouble. Our link to that supernatural resource can only be made through faith. When we've strengthened our spiritual muscles through God's Word, then we'll be able to handle life's curve balls because we'll remember and believe the encouragement from His Word:

- *"'No weapon forged against you will prevail, and you will refute every tongue that accuses you. This is the heritage of the servants of the LORD, and this is their vindication from me,' declares the LORD."* (Isaiah 54:17 NIV)

- *"Despite all these things, overwhelming victory is ours through Christ, who loved us. And I am convinced that nothing can ever separate us from his love. Death can't, and life can't. The angels can't, and the demons can't. Our fears for today, our worries about tomorrow, and even the powers of hell can't keep God's love away. Whether we are high above the sky or in the deepest ocean, nothing in all creation will ever be able to separate us from the love of God that is revealed in Christ Jesus our Lord."* (Romans 8:37–39 NLT)

- *"We have small troubles for a while now, but they are helping us gain an eternal glory. That glory is much greater than the troubles. So we set our eyes not on what we see but on what we cannot see. What we see will last only a short time. But what we cannot see will last forever."* (2 Corinthians 4:17–18 ICB)

We belong to God, and we can live with an eternal perspective that recognizes God's hand at work in every aspect of our lives—good as well as bad. Our hope is not in this life. We've traded our self-driven dreams of the here and now for heaven's dreams with their roots in eternity. That's why we can shrug off the disappointments of this world with the attitude of Job: "Shall we indeed accept good from God, and shall we not accept adversity?" (Job 2:10). Job understood this truth: "Naked I came from my mother's womb, and naked shall I return there. The LORD gave, and the LORD has taken away; blessed be the name of the LORD" (Job 1:21).

But we cannot echo the faith of Job's words if we haven't first experienced the miracle of God's power to save us from ourselves. Through the supernatural work of Christ's death on the cross, God reestablished His connection with us that was lost in the Fall. When Adam and Eve sinned, they became separated from God. They died. In Christ we are reconnected—or as the Bible puts it, born again. We live. We needed to be born again because we were spiritually dead: "You were spiritually dead because of your sins and because you were not free from the power of your sinful self. But God made you alive with Christ. And God forgave all our sins" (Colossians 2:13 ICB).

> We've traded our self-driven dreams of the here and now for heaven's dreams with their roots in eternity.

God not only forgave us for our sins, He also freed us from the power of sin itself: "Sin is no longer your master, for you are no longer subject to the law, which enslaves you to sin. Instead, you are free by God's grace" (Romans 6:14 NLT). This is one of the things we learn as we study God's Word, and it's vital to know because sin is what Satan uses to try to keep us from God and His Word.

I would be remiss if I didn't reveal one more piece of the puzzle by defining sin. I think it may surprise some to know that sin simply means missing the mark. Sin is anything that takes us away from God's best for us. When we walk in our own ways and according to our own plans and thoughts, we're missing God's mark. We are, in biblical terms, sinning.

The Bible explains, "When you offer yourselves to someone to obey him as slaves, you are slaves to the one whom you obey—whether you are slaves to sin, which leads to death, or to obedience, which leads to righteousness" (Romans 6:16 NIV). We can't follow our sinful desires and still serve God. Satan knows this and uses it against us. We must choose to obey God, but if we don't know that we've been freed from sin, we might think we don't have a choice. The apostle Paul wrote:

Nothing good lives in me—I mean nothing good lives in the part of me that is earthly and sinful. I want to do the things that are good. But I do not do them. I do not do the good things that I want to do. I do the bad things that I do not want to do. So if I do things I do not want to do, then I am not the one doing those things. It is sin living in me that does those bad things.

So I have learned this rule: When I want to do good, evil is there with me. In my mind, I am happy with God's law. But I see another law working in my body. That law makes war against the law that my mind accepts. That other law working in my body is the law of sin, and that law makes me its prisoner. What a miserable man I am! Who will save me from this body that brings me death? (Romans 7:18–24 ICB)

This miserable condition is where we can find ourselves when we don't know the rest of the story. Without the full counsel of God, we don't know that we don't have to remain in this state of frustration. Paul gave us the answer to the question "Who will save me from this body that brings me death?":

God will. I thank him for saving me through Jesus Christ our Lord!

So in my mind I am a slave to God's law. But in my sinful self I am a slave to the law of sin.

So now, those who are in Christ Jesus are not judged guilty. I am not judged guilty because in Christ Jesus the law of the Spirit that brings life made me free. It made me free from the law that brings sin and death. The law was without power, because the law was made weak by our sinful selves. But God did what the law could not do. He sent his own Son to earth with the same human life that others use for sin. He sent his Son to be an offering to pay for sin. So God used a human life to destroy sin. He did this so that we could be right as the law said we must be. Now we do not live following our sinful selves, but we live following the Spirit. (Romans 7:25–8:4 ICB)

Sin keeps us from realizing heaven's dreams and walking in the supernatural power of God. But God's Word grants us the faith to take hold of what is ours as children of God and to walk free from sin's power, offering a miraculous witness to the world.

The Goal of God's Word

God's Word is a vital part of our day-to-day existence because it tells us what the mark is. We still have to choose to reach for the goal, but at least we know what we're aiming at. It gives us that goal about which Paul wrote:

I do not mean that I am already as God wants me to be. I have not yet reached that goal. But I continue trying to reach it and to make it mine. Christ wants me to do that. That is the reason Christ made me his. Brothers, I know that I have not yet reached that goal. But there is one thing I always do: I forget the things that are past. I try as hard as I can to reach the goal that is before me. I keep trying to reach the goal and get the prize. That prize is mine because God called me through Christ to the life above. (Philippians 3:12–14 ICB)

God has called us to perfection. We may not reach the goal in this life, but our whole journey is designed to put us on the path toward that goal and its eternal prize.

In hindsight we can readily see that Joseph achieved that goal to a much greater degree than his brothers did. Through every trial and test, Joseph's faith grew to the point where he was walking in his God-given dream with enough provision to share his abundance, power to save others, and a position from which to shine forth the excellence of what God had accomplished in and through him.

What about you? Are you weary of trying to make your dreams come true with your own limited resources? Could you use a supernatural boost? Can you relate to Paul on the road to Damascus, when Jesus asked him if he was getting tired of fighting against Him? (see Acts 9:5). Does your heart leap with hope when you read the following words of Jesus? "Come to me, all of you who are tired and have heavy loads. I will give you rest. Accept my work and learn from me. I am gentle and humble in spirit. And you will find rest for your souls. The work that I ask you to accept is easy. The load I give you to carry is not heavy" (Matthew 11:28–30 ICB).

If you answered yes to these questions, then answer one more. Are you willing to spend time daily in God's Word to build your faith to the point that you can begin to see His supernatural working in your life through the natural course of events? If so, you'll find the joy and relief of being able to trust your dream to an almighty God who has the power and the desire to make that dream come true.

When we place whatever we have in the Master's hands, He will bless and multiply it. We'll find ourselves in the midst of an unusual and significant event orchestrated by a supernatural agent for the purpose of authenticating the message that we are God's peculiar people—chosen to belong to Him alone.

This supernatural existence will put us in positions to shine—where excellence, the third characteristic of a God-given dream, will manifest itself.

When heaven's dreams become our realities, we'll find God living His dream in and through us. We'll walk in the abundance of His provision and in the supernatural power of His strength.

an excellent *dream*

Since we have two young children, one of our family's favorite vacation spots is Walt Disney World in Orlando, Florida. Although this amazing resort offers endless fun and enjoyment, I'm most impressed with the excellence I encounter in the Magic Kingdom. I've often pondered how much greater our reaction will be to the wonder and awe we'll feel when we finally enter the kingdom of heaven.

Everything that is good on this earth is but a reflection of the excellence of God. For us to appreciate how much that excellence will impact our lives through heaven's dreams, it's important to explore the truth of God's excellence—because when we are linked heart to heart, mind to mind, soul to soul, and spirit to Spirit with God, His brilliance, distinction, and perfection will be displayed in our lives. We will be reflections of His excellence.

The Perfection of God's Work

Excellence is one of the distinguishing marks of a God-given dream. From art's most magnificent masterpiece to the awe-inspiring performance of a

225

gold–medal-winning athlete, we get a glimpse of the perfection of God—in whose image we were created.

When God created the earth, the plants, animals, and the first man and woman, He made them in the perfection of His own character and declared them to be very good (see Genesis 1:31). But through the disobedience of Adam and Eve, the creation was marred by sin. So when we encounter excellence, it resonates with that part of the human soul that longs for the perfection from which it fell.

God created us for fellowship with Him. We were meant to be eternally involved in an ongoing love relationship with God, who would sustain us in an infinite state of perfection. But we were ambushed by the Enemy when he successfully lured Adam and Eve to step outside the protective boundary of God's provision and love. Once they were separated from God, sin and death took their toll until Christ paid the penalty for sin and redeemed humankind from the bondage of sin and death. That's why when we surrender our sinful, death-ridden lives apart from Christ to God through Christ, God reestablishes the connection that was lost so long ago. In Christ all of God's excellence is once again available to flow in and through us. The writer of Hebrews affirmed this: "With one sacrifice he made perfect forever those who are being made holy" (Hebrews 10:14 ICB).

> In Christ all of God's excellence is once again available to flow in and through us.

What is this excellence that will flow through us from God? I would have to write another book even to scratch the surface, but for fun I want to share just a few of the things that make God so extraordinary.

Even though God is Spirit and cannot be seen, we can know about Him from nature. A modern translation of the Bible says, "The basic reality of God is plain enough. Open your eyes and there it is! By taking a long and thoughtful look at what God has created, people have always been able to see what their eyes as such can't see: eternal power, for instance, and the mystery of his divine being" (Romans 1:19–20 The Message).

God's handiwork is so excellent that Ric Ergenbright, in *The Art of God*, likened God's creation to a work of art:

> The art of God was created by the Word of God, spoken outside of time and space, possessing the inherent power to bring forth visible physical matter from invisible spiritual energy. Hence, all that exists, from the whole of the cosmos to its subatomic particles, bears the clear impression of God. . . .
>
> Because *all things* are the work of His hands, and nothing exists that He has not made, it is commonplace for us to take God's art for granted, or even to believe the critic who says it's really not art at all, but rather something that just happened—a serendipitous accident that simply stumbled into existence through a mindless meeting of time and chance.
>
> Were this said of the *Mona Lisa* or the Sistine Chapel we would think it totally absurd. Why then, when even the simplest molecule in nature is infinitely more complex and perfect than those masterworks by da Vinci and Michelangelo, do we give less credence to the higher art form and spurn its Designer and Creator?[1]

Put in these terms, it's hard to argue with the excellence of God in nature, but what about the excellence of God displayed in the human body? The psalmist wrote, "I will praise You, for I am fearfully and wonderfully made; marvelous are Your works, and that my soul knows very well" (Psalm 139:14). In an article entitled "Exploring the Mind of Man: The Human Brain," Chuck Missler presented these mind-boggling facts concerning the human brain:

It has been estimated that the brain is composed of 10^{10} nerve cells, each with 10^4–10^5 connecting fibers, thus approaching 10^{15} separate connections.

How can we grasp this complexity? In order to imagine a 10^{15} equivalent, try to imagine a forest half the size of the United States—about 1 million square miles. Assume there were 10,000 trees per square mile, each with 100,000 leaves on each tree. That's a bunch. That's 10^{15} leaves. . . .

If only 1% of the connections were specifically organized pathways, it would still represent a greater number of connections than the entire communications network on the Planet Earth! . . .

The brilliant physicist and mathematician, John von Neumann, once calculated that over the course of the average human lifetime, the brain stores something on the order of 2.8×10^{20} bits of information. (Applying the traditional estimate of the age of the universe as about 10 billion years, that's 1,000 bits for every second in the entire history of the universe!)[2]

Now, with these complex brains we have, let's think about this statement from an article on human DNA, "Unraveling DNA's Design," by Dr. Jerry Bergman: "At the moment of conception, a fertilized human egg is about the size of a pinhead. Yet it contains information equivalent to about six billion 'chemical letters.' This is enough information to fill 1,000 books, 500 pages thick with print so small you would need a microscope to read it! If all the chemical 'letters' in the human body were printed in books, it is estimated they would fill the Grand Canyon fifty times!"[3]

While we're trying to read all those books, let's take into consideration these facts about the eyes we're using to read them, from *The World, the Word & You*:

When light reflected from an object of sight enters a human eye, it passes through the cornea, the pupil and the lens, and lands on the retina. The retina contains two kinds of light detecting cells. These cells are called rods and cones. The cones are color sensors, and the rods make night vision possible. The retina is paper-thin, but contains about 130 billion light receptors. Around 6 million of these are the "cones" which allow us to see some 8 million different colors. The remaining 124 million rods only detect black and white reflected light. These rods are crucial for the human eye and allow night vision. You see, once the human eye adjusts to darkness, these rods become 75,000 times more sensitive, allowing us to see very dimly lit objects and movements.

Now eyes in various creatures which God has made, vary greatly in makeup. It appears God designed eyes to meet the differing needs of each creature's environment. For instance, human beings need excellent resolution for detail work, so God designed the human eye for detail. But, the pesky fly that buzzes us during the summer months has a different eye and need. Since the fly needs speed as we all know, its eye is designed to see images at ultra high speed. A fly can detect a flicker of 200 Hz, versus the human eye at 10 Hz, which would allow it to see our conventional movies as slide shows! This enables the fly to be one step ahead of your attempts to catch it or swat it by the movement of your hand.[4]

I don't know about you, but it is difficult for me as a thinking, intelligent human being to believe that something as sophisticated as my eye could have evolved by chance to such a level of complexity. And how is it that the fly's eye evolved differently?

Doctors, scientists, and researchers have recently been elated to create an artificial heart, yet the heart is one of the least complicated organs in the human body. I don't believe that even if we lived one hundred million years more, we would be able to reproduce the brain or the nervous system.

Divine Completion

I've given only a few brief examples from the universe and the human body, but I believe they adequately make the point of God's superiority, brilliance, distinction, and perfection. It is this God who invites us to receive His perfect plans for our lives. When we do finally surrender our measly, limited, self-driven dreams, He gives us His abundant, supernatural, excellent dreams. Our journey is complete because our connection with the Creator is reestablished, and it's that completion that brings excellence. But our journey is far from finished.

We tend to think that when something is complete, it's over and done with—finished. But with God the dream is never over, because life is eternal. The journey is not about accomplishing the dream but about reconnecting to God so the dream can continue eternally in the excellence for which it was designed.

Unfortunately, many potential dreamers never make it because they miss the eternal nature of the dream. They miss the greater purpose in this life—finding the Dream Giver. Jesus said we must "enter through the narrow gate. The road that leads to hell is a very easy road. And the gate to hell is very wide. Many people enter through that gate. But the gate that opens the way to true life is very small. And the road to true life is very hard. Only a few people find that road" (Matthew 7:13–14 ICB).

Those who enter through that narrow gate that leads to true life are those who have surrendered their own lives in exchange for the supernatural life of Christ. They've learned the lessons of the pit, the marketplace, and the prison. They have gained hearts of wisdom to handle the abundance of heaven's dreams. And they've started walking in excellence on this adventure of faith. They search no longer for the dream. They are content to walk day by day, moment by moment in the provision of the One to whom they belong. They have attained that eternal perspective that is hailed in the Hebrews Hall of Faith:

All these great men died in faith. They did not get the things that God promised his people. But they saw them coming far in the future and were glad. They said that they were like visitors and strangers on earth. When people say such things, then they show that they are looking for a country that will be their own country. If they had been thinking about that country they had left, they could have gone back. But those men were waiting for a better country—a heavenly country. So God is not ashamed to be called their God. For he has prepared a city for them. (Hebrews 11:13–16 ICB)

The journey is not about accomplishing the dream but about reconnecting to God so the dream can continue eternally in the excellence for which it was designed.

These men and women lived by faith. Their dreams were not limited to their lives on earth. They transcended their mortality by connecting to Him who is immortal. That's where we leave Joseph at the end of his life—in the Hall of Faith: "It was by faith that Joseph spoke about the Israelites leaving Egypt while he was dying. He told them what to do with his body" (Hebrews 11:22 ICB).

Joseph had a dream, and as he journeyed through the pit, the marketplace, and the prison, his dream proved to be God-given. He started out as a cocky, young, independent dreamer, but he ended up a wise, seasoned, God-dependent dreamer. He had learned to see the unseen.

Some folks look at Calvary Chapel Fort Lauderdale today and say to me, "Wow! That's excellent!" I never want to come across as boastful, but it's true that on the charts of what's considered big, we're up there. Our congregation of around eighteen thousand people reflects the cultural makeup of our community. Our more than four-hundred-thousand-square-foot facility stands on roughly eighty acres of property. That's what Calvary Chapel Fort Lauderdale looks like today, but that's not how it looked when it started.

The story started when I was an associate pastor at Calvary Chapel Las Vegas for two years. One of my responsibilities was teaching in a Sunday-afternoon service for around four hundred people. I was also part of a group that got together and prayed over the prayer requests from people in the church body.

During one of those prayer meetings, I read a request to pray that God would send a pastor to start a Calvary Chapel in Fort Lauderdale. I didn't think much of it until I began to pray and the words started to echo in my head and heart like they were coming from the hallways of heaven. I left the meeting undone. I knew that I had felt a supernatural calling, but I wasn't sure I was up for it.

That night Diane and I went out for ice cream, and I told her that I thought God was calling us to Fort Lauderdale, Florida. As it would happen, right outside the ice-cream parlor was a travel agency. We decided to go in and look at a map to get a better feel for exactly where Fort Lauderdale was. Diane ran her finger from California, her home state, all the way across the United States and down the state of Florida, almost to the tip, until it rested on the dot labeled Fort Lauderdale. "Wow," she said. "That's a long way from home."

In spite of our initial hesitation, we both began to pray. We told no one, so it was quite a shock when Diane's prayer partner approached her and said, "Hey, are you guys going to start a church in Fort Lauderdale?" It was one of those supernatural events I told you about that had become a part of my life once I became a Christian. After several more confirmations from Scripture, we knew that we were Fort Lauderdale bound. But getting there was not uneventful, nor were we free of doubt.

chapter 12: an excellent *dream*

Even after we arrived in Fort Lauderdale, I thought, *I know I'm a pastor, but I don't know if I'm going to start a Sunday-morning service yet. I don't know if I'm ready for that.* God had put the dream in my heart, but now that I was actually walking on a path that looked like it might happen, I was fearful. This was a very different fear from the pit. This wasn't a fear that the dream wouldn't come true but rather that it would. In spite of my doubts and fears, I persevered through the first two years.

My expectation was never that the church would be huge, but I had hoped it would be healthy. So you can imagine how taken aback I was with the first few folks the Lord sent my direction. They were colorful critics, to say the least. I remember one gentleman named Red who chewed tobacco as he stood outside the door during the whole service so he could spit on the ground every couple of minutes. Of course, it didn't matter much because our "sanctuary" was the living room of an eight-hundred-square-foot house with no air conditioning. In the middle of a sweltering Florida summer, at least the open door allowed a breeze to pass through.

We held a Tuesday-night Bible study at that house. The group was comprised of everyone and anyone who showed up as a result of the fliers we were handing out at the beach. Many of those first visitors were just looking for a handout and not really into the Bible-study part of the deal. This left me, after the study, doing exasperating things like debating the finer points of Freemasonry with Red between chews. I wasn't sure what I had expected when I came to Fort Lauderdale, but I was pretty sure that wasn't it.

I guess if I were to be totally honest, I was expecting something great, and I don't think that's necessarily wrong. When we dream, we should dream big. What would be the point of pursuing a mediocre dream? Our dreams should shoot for the moon, not settle for humdrum.

We all strive for greatness because we are created in the image of a great God. This brings us back to the reason God spends so much time conforming the character of the dreamer into the image of His Son, Jesus. Only when our character begins to conform to Christ's can we see the excellence of God's life in the seemingly mundane and ordinary details of life on earth.

That's what happened to me. When I made that call to Calvary Chapel Costa Mesa after two years of pastoring in Fort Lauderdale, I was ready to quit. After that call I surrendered everything to God. I didn't get a megachurch right away, but I did get in step with an infinite God through whom I began to realize the dream of excellence. And from that point forward, the church grew.

The Exchange for Excellence

The Bible says, "Sing to the LORD, for He has done excellent things; this is known in all the earth" (Isaiah 12:5). Why then do so many Christians fall short of being known as excellent? The general public seems to have lost the expectation for Christians to have a reputation for excellence. The media often portrays Christians as buffoons and religious weirdos.

What happened to the excellent spirit that would be known in all the earth? Something happened. Somewhere along the way, God's people seem to have forgotten that they belong to Him and that He is excellent.

We've forgotten because the devil has effectively kept us from the truth of God's Word. Many churches don't teach it anymore. Intellectuals dismiss it as narrow-minded in a society that values tolerance and inclusiveness. Scientists attempt to discredit its claims of the miraculous as unprovable. Yet the Bible is where we discover that "the LORD of hosts . . . is wonderful in counsel and excellent in guidance" (Isaiah 28:29). The only way to bring back the expression of excellence in our lives as believers is for us to follow the excellent guidance set out in God's Word. Since we have an excellent God who is leading us in an excellent way, the fruit of accepting His way will be personal excellence.

At this point I have to ask: Are you going to settle for the status quo, or are you willing to step out in faith on a quest with God for excellence? What will you have to remove from your life in order to make way for the excellence of God?

If you have a dream to be married, are you in a relationship now that is not God's best? Are you willing to let go of your mediocre, self-driven dream in exchange for your excellent, God-given dream? If you ever expect Mr. or Ms. Right to show up, Mr. or Ms. Wrong is going to have to go.

Are you in a business that's limping along? Are you expending every extra ounce of energy and resources to keep that self-driven dream alive? How about letting it die so that God can bring the excellence of His plan into this area of your life. God is not in the business of taking from us without purpose. He's in the business of restoration and redemption. That includes giving us back a dream that's even better than our own self-driven dreams.

> At this point I have to ask: Are you going to settle for the status quo, or are you willing to step out in faith on a quest with God for excellence?

He is the God who owns the cattle on a thousand hills (see Psalm 50:10), who owns everything under heaven (see Job 41:11), who has blessed us with every spiritual blessing in Christ Jesus (see Ephesians 1:3), who is all-knowing (see 1 John 3:20), all-powerful (see Matthew 28:18; 1 Peter 5:11; Revelation 19:6), gracious, benevolent, merciful, long-suffering, and abounding in goodness and truth (see Exodus 34:6). Do you really think He would take away your business and leave you with nothing?

May I remind you, as you are making the important decision of whether to trust this same God with your dreams, that above all else that He is, He is madly in love with you. I'm not suggesting you surrender to a deity that couldn't care less. God's love is so profound that He left praise and adoration in heaven to come to earth and endure hatred and rejection. He died a brutal death on the cross just so He could offer you His dream right now. The Bible explains:

- *"God loved the world so much that he gave his only Son. God gave his Son so that whoever believes in him may not be lost, but have eternal life." (John 3:16 ICB)*

- *"Christ died for us while we were still sinners. In this way God shows his great love for us." (Romans 5:8 ICB)*

- *"Christ died for all so that those who live would not continue to live for themselves. He died for them and was raised from death so that they would live for him." (2 Corinthians 5:15 ICB)*

- *"What can we say about such wonderful things as these? If God is for us, who can ever be against us? Since God did not spare even his own Son but gave him up for us all, won't God, who gave us Christ, also give us everything else?" (Romans 8:31–32 NLT)*

God is love, and everything He does is motivated by His love. It's like the love a parent has for a child. That kind of love motivates us to do great things for our kids. Diane went shopping this week to buy the ingredients for next week's meals. The food is already in the pantry, and the kids haven't had to think about it or worry at all what they will eat. I've planned a vacation for our family. I already know where we'll go. I know the place where we'll stay. I've thought about the boat we'll rent and the lake we'll fish from. I have an entire adventure planned, but my kids still have no clue. And I won't reveal it to them until we go, because I want it to unfold as a blessing for them one day at a time.

That's how God's love works for us, His children. "'I know what I have planned for you,' says the Lord. 'I have good plans for you. I don't plan to hurt you. I plan to give you hope and a good future'" (Jeremiah 29:11 ICB).

This is the opposite of our mistaken conception of a God who is so busy in the heavenly realm that He can't take time out even to think about us. We somehow picture Him with a fax machine running non-stop, His cell phone ringing off the hook, and millions of people in His waiting room. We imagine Him deluged with world catastrophes to tend and world-shaping decisions to make. We conclude that our chances for getting an appointment with Him would be slim to none.

In reality it's the other way around. It's God who has a hard time getting us to spend any time with Him because our fax machines are running, our cell phones are ringing, and we're busy with the people in our lives. We've elevated our diminutive life situations to the self-important level of world crises.

God would love to spend a few minutes with us to tell us about the plans He has for us. If we took the time to hear Him, we would find out that He wants to make us into the kind of Christian described by J. I. Packer in his book *Knowing God*:

> What is a Christian? He can be described from many angles, but . . . we can cover everything by saying: he is a man who acknowledges and lives under the word of God. He submits without reserve to the word of God written in 'the Scripture of truth' (Daniel 10:21), believing the teaching, trusting the promises, following the commands. His eyes are to the God of the Bible as his Father, and the Christ of the Bible as his Saviour. He will tell you, if you ask him, that the word of God has both convinced him of sin and assured him of forgiveness. His conscience, like Luther's, is captive to the word of God, and he aspires, like the psalmist, to have his whole life

brought into line with it. . . . (Psalm 119:5, 10, 26, 36, 80). The promises are before him as he prays, and the precepts are before him as he moves among men. He knows that in addition to the word of God spoken directly to him in the Scriptures, God's word has also gone forth to create, and control, and order things around him; but since the Scriptures tell him that all things work together for his good, the thought of God ordering his circumstances brings him only joy. He is an independent fellow, for he uses the word of God as a touchstone by which to test the various views that are put to him, and he will not touch anything which he is not sure that Scripture sanctions.[5]

Does this describe your life? If not, it's time to choose: will you let go of your own dream and allow heaven's dream to become your reality? The ball is in your court. I pray you will complete the journey by connecting with the Dream Giver. Then you can know the abundant provision, supernatural power, and shining excellence of a God-given dream. At last you'll be living a dreamality.

While it's true that every individual has a dream, it's also true that every dream worth pursuing has one common denominator. We alluded to that unique thread in chapter 2: our chief end, our purpose, is to glorify God and enjoy Him forever. So wherever you are in your journey—whether you're in the pit, doubting the reality of the dream in the first place; or the marketplace, where your dream looks like it may be up for grabs; or behind bars, where you can see your dream in the distance but think you'll never attain it—let me leave you with this word of assurance. God wants to make heaven's dream your reality so that you can glorify Him and enjoy His presence forever.

I think it was the frustration of not being able to give my daughter her dream back that motivated me to write this book. If it had been humanly possible to do so, I would have gone to the moon and back to give Caitlyn whatever her heart desired that morning. God is certainly not a lesser parent than I am, but God didn't go to the moon to get our dreams back for us. He came to Earth. Unlike me, God not only *wants* to give us our dreams, He is *able* to do so. I want more than anything for you to know the heavenly Father who can and will give you more than you could ever imagine possible.

Remember all those promises that are ours by faith? One of them goes like this: "Eye has not seen, nor ear heard, nor have entered into the heart of man the things which God has prepared for those who love

Him" (1 Corinthians 2:9). It's a promise that God has good things in store for us if we'll just trust Him.

As I look back over the last twenty-three years that I've known this awesome and magnificent God I call Father, Savior, and Friend, I can honestly say that the truth of this verse has been unequivocally proven beyond all my feeble doubts and fears. Please don't think, however, that God did extraordinary things in my life because I'm someone special. That would be a mistake. I'm just like you—a human being, flawed and frail. What sets me apart is not the dream God has fulfilled in my life but the fact that I have chosen to belong to a dream-giving God. And that's a choice you can make too.

It is my prayer that through the pages of this book, you will be encouraged to seek the same heavenly Father I have. He's the only One powerful enough, wise enough, and good enough to restore and fulfill heaven's dream in your life.

introduction: everybody *dreams*

1. "Modern Scotland: Eric Liddell wins gold, 1924," BBC, http://www.bbc.co.uk/history/timelines/scotland/eric_liddell.shtml (accessed March 21, 2005).

2. W. David O. Taylor, "In Defense of Mere Entertainment (Part 3)," ChristianityToday.com, http://www.christianitytoday.com/movies/commentaries /mereentertainment.html (accessed March 21, 2005).

chapter 2: provision to *share*

1. "Westminster Catechism," Encyclopædia Britannica Premium Service, http://www.britannica.com/eb/article?tocId=9076687 (accessed March 21, 2005).

2. Empty Tomb, Inc., http://www.emptytomb.org/lifestylestat.php (accessed March 3, 2005).

3. "Reaching Out in Love to the Suffering of Iraq," North Carolina Conference of Missions, http://nccumc.org/missions/iraq_ministry.htm (accessed March 3, 2005).

4. "Crazy, huh?" Duncanville Church of Christ, http://www.duncanvillechurch .com/ronsarticles/crazyhuh.htm (accessed March 3, 2005).

5. "John D. Rockefeller Quotes," BrainyQuote, http://www.brainyquote.com /quotes/authors/j/john_d_rockefeller.html (accessed March 17, 2005).

6. Sonja Steptoe, "The Man with the Purpose," *Time*, March 29, 2004.

7. Mark Water, comp., *The New Encyclopedia of Christian Quotations* (Grand Rapids: Baker Books, 2000), 401.

8. William H. Terry, "Virtues for Living" (sermon, Covenant Presbyterian Church, Charlotte, N.C., January 11, 2004), http://www.covenantpresby.org/SermonArchive.htm (accessed March 9, 2005).

chapter 3: power to *save*

1. *The American Heritage Dictionary of the English Language*, 4th ed., s.v. "salvation."

2. "Jake's Story, the Battle of a Teen," *My God Story* (Fort Lauderdale, Fla.: Calvary Chapel Church, Inc., 2001), 57–61.

chapter 5: the hate behind the *nightmare*

1. "Asleep in the Light" written by Keith Green. ©Birdwing Music/BMG Songs/Ears to Hear Music (Admin. By EMI CMG) All Rights Reserved. Used by Permission.

2. A. W. Tozer, *Born After Midnight* (Harrisburg, Pa.: Christian Publications, 1959), 43.

chapter 7: the *marketplace*

1. Werner Gift, "Counting the Stars," *Creation Magazine*, http://www.answeringenesis.org/creation/v19/i2/stars.asp?vPrint=1 (accessed March 23, 2005).

2. "A Bicycle Built for Two" in *My God Story* (Fort Lauderdale, Fla.: Calvary Chapel Church, Inc., 2001), 130–32.

3. Mark Eastman and Chuck Smith, *The Search for Messiah*, rev. ed. (n.p.: Joy Publishing, 1996), 61.

chapter 10: an abundant *dream*

1. Mike Cleveland, author, founder, and president of Setting Captives Free, http://www.settingcaptivesfree.com.

chapter 11: a supernatural *dream*

1. Hampton Keathley IV, Th.M., "Introduction to the Miracles of Jesus," http://www.bible.org/page.asp?page_id=2212 (accessed March 18, 2005).

2. "National Infant Immunization Week, April 16–22," news release by the Maryland Department of Health and Mental Hygiene, April 14, 2000,

http://www.dhmh.state.md.us/publ-rel/html/immunwee.htm (accessed March 18, 2005).

chapter 12: an excellent *dream*

1. Ric Ergenbright, *The Art of God* (Wheaton, Ill.: Tyndale House Publishers, 1999), 21.

2. Chuck Missler, "Exploring the Mind of Man: The Human Brain," http://www.khouse.org/articles/1999/229 (accessed March 18, 2005). This article was excerpted from *Cosmic Codes—Hidden Messages from the Edge of Eternity.* Originally published in *Personal Update News Journal*, February 1999.

3. Dr. Jerry Bergman, "Unraveling DNA's Design," Koinonia House Online, http://www.khouse.org/articles/1997/143 (accessed March 18, 2005). Originally published in *Personal Update News Journal*, December 1997.

4. Dennis L. Finnan, "The Eyes Have It," *The World, the Word & You!* Christian Radio Broadcast, http://www.finnan.org/wwy1304.html (accessed March 18, 2005).

5. J. I. Packer, *Knowing God* (Downer's Grove, Ill.: InterVarsity Press, 1973), 104–105.